THE THIRD MAN ON THE GALLOWS

Michael W. Dewar

Copyright © 2025 by Michael W. Dewar
THE THIRD MAN ON THE GALLOWS

ISBN: 979-8-9883484-2-9 (Paperback)
ISBN: 979-8-9928854-0-8 (eBook)

Published by Dwelling Place Publishers
Brooklyn, New York 11236
United States of America
DPSCleansing.com

All rights reserved solely by the author. The author guarantees all contents are original and do not infringe upon the legal rights of any other person or work. No part of this book may be reproduced in any form without the permission of the author.

Unless otherwise indicated, Bible quotations are taken from The Holy Bible, New International Version(NIV). Copyright © 1973, 1978, 1984 by International Bible Society; The Holy Bible, King James Version(KJV or NKJV); and The Holy Bible, New Living Translation(NLT). Copyright © 1996 by Tyndale House Publishers, Inc.

CONTENTS

Preface..v

Introduction..7

Chapter 1 The Divine Choreography........................13

Chapter 2 The Two Thieves....................................25

Chapter 3 The Nazarene's Response to a Thief...........39

Chapter 4 The Trip tp Paradise................................49

Chapter 5 The Biblical Underworld...........................65

Chapter 6 The Return from Paradise........................75

Chapter 7 The Transfer of Paradise..........................89

Reference..101

Other Books by This Author...................................103

About the Author..105

If you are lost, follow the Son.

PREFACE

While this book is for all seasons of the year, and all cycles of a person's life, it has a particular relevance to the Lent and Easter season.

If you never had the chance to focus on the three central characters executed on that Friday, we now call Good Friday, this work will make a delightful read for the season. It will help you to experience more deeply the mystery of what took place that day. That earthshaking event has resonated with time and has impacted and transformed billions of lives for time and eternity.

This is the first in a series of books intitled, "Witnesses to an Execution." One or more will be released each year in time for the Lent and Easter season, if the Lord wills it.

The book is a good supplemental read for the divinity student in the academy, but it was not written for the academy. It was written for the average, everyday person in the pews of our places of worship. That could be a cathedral, a store front church, a gathering at home, under a tree in the park, or a hut in some faraway places. The Nazarene promised to be present whenever and wherever two or three people come together in His name (Matthew 18:20).

This is a work written to connect the followers of the Nazarene more deeply to the sacrifice offered for all of us on that hillside so long ago. The author invites you to read and reflect on that supreme sacrifice that hung on the middle gallows.

INTRODUCTION

It was a Friday morning, a Spring Day in the year AD 33 in Jerusalem. Three men condemned to death by the Roman authorities, were ceremonially marched through the narrow, cobble stone streets of the city under the weight of their own gallows to the place of execution outside the ancient city.

The streets dutifully lined with spectators and sympathizers, helplessly looking on, curious and afraid, some gleefully mocking, others weeping, sobbing, mothers wailing. Soldiers, some on horseback, others on foot, armed with spares, swords, and shields, pushed back the crowd as the procession made its way to the execution site. It was a barren, skull-shaped hill outside the city; some called it Golgotha, others Calvary (Matthew 27:33).

The man that was later placed on the middle gallows was a popular, itinerant preacher and healer named,

Yeshua, came from the peasant village of Nazareth. Some just refer to Him as the Nazarene. The other two men were nameless thieves, but no ordinary thieves; they were charged with sedition against the Roman State. As the procession advanced toward Golgotha, the Nazarene, weakened from severe scourging and loss of blood, fell beneath the weight of the gallows he was shouldering. The soldiers compelled a stranger named Simon of Syrine to help the Nazarene (Matthew 27: 32).

While the Nazarene is pivotal to this story, the focus is on all three men; each has a story critical to what happened that day. However, we only know about the two thieves because of their encounter with the Nazarene that fateful day. Otherwise, they would have been lost to history like many others who had suffered the same fate.

The biography of these two men are unknown, except that they were thieves. One may ask, what is so important about them? Well, the fact that we are talking about them two-thousand years later suggests their importance to the story; that alone is enough to stir one's curiosity.

It is often said that "no man comes into this world by himself," and "no one dies by himself." Just as the man on the middle gallows had a family, friends, acquaintances, and sympathizers watching him die that day, chances are—the other two men also had families and supporters quietly, helplessly, looking on as well.

But as criminals and disgraced sons, it was better for their families and well-wishers to remain faceless and hidden in the crowd for their safety. Shame and fear of reprisal kept them unidentified. For the same reason, most of the Nazarene's immediate followers were not present at the site of execution. They were afraid too and chose hiding instead. But not all, present were John, a close friend and follower of the Nazarene, and Mary the mother of the Nazarene, Mary's sister, Mary the wife of Clopas, and Mary Magdalene (John 19: 25).

If no one else wanted to be there, the mothers that birthed these two misguided young men would have wanted to be there above all else. And perhaps they were very much there, standing in painful grief, sobbing with the mother of the Nazarene. Helpless they were, unable to do anything. Of the three men, the Nazarene was placed on the middle gallows.

But what a contrast, three mothers! Two gave birth to sons who became criminals, one that gave birth to a Son who became Savior, Lord, Redeemer. But for now, they are just grieving mothers trying to make sense of this strange irony—the best of men dying the same fate as the worst of men. That's how it appeared to those who were unable to see the hand of God in this scandalous drama.

Little did they know that they were all making history that day. Mothers two thousand years removed would want to train their sons to follow the example of the man on the middle gallows and stay clear of the path the others took.

The Purpose of this Book

It is commonly accepted that human nature remains the same from time immemorial. There is the need for survival, food, shelter, security, and pleasure. Within that context, the purpose of this book is three-fold.

First, to discuss the lives of these three men and extrapolate from them what edifies, and what can inform the ordering of our lives in the twenty-first century and beyond. For good or evil, we can all find ourselves in the story of one of these three men.

Second, our purpose is to pull back the curtains of eternity for a sneak glimpse of what is moving toward us, and how to best prepare for it as one thief did that day. All of us during our journey of life will come to a similar intersection of destiny, when we are called upon to make the correct destination choice. Will we be as discerning and discriminating as the penitent thief was? Or spiritually blind as his partner in crime?

The third purpose of this book is to examine the validity of the claim, that all human beings can have a blessed hope and a future, if a relationship is established before death with the man on the middle gallows.

One thief, at the most critical juncture of his life, established that positive relationship, and indeed secured for himself a hope and a future. But the other thief made the opposite choice with a regrettable outcome.

Come with me to this place of execution where we can see the three gallows more clearly, observe the behavior of these men more intentionally, and listen to what they are saying more carefully. We may gain insights into some of the pitfalls of life to avoid and the wisdom to order our pilgrimage more fruitfully.

INTRODUCTION

But one more thing, I must warn you that this journey on which you are invited is not for the faint-hearted. It will take you from the frightening place of execution through the gates of Sheol (hell), Paradise, heaven, and back. The experience will be most rewarding, and you will be better for having taken this journey.

One of the questions you may want to consider on your journey is this—was the death of the Nazarene accidental, coincidental, or providential? Framed another way, was this scandalous drama an accident of history or divinely choreographed? Keep your answer to the end of the journey when you can better draw a more informed conclusion.

If you lost your way, follow the Son.

CHAPTER 1

THE DIVINE CHOREOGRAPHY

The purpose of this chapter is to show that nothing in the context of the Nazarene's life and death was accidental, coincidental, or left to sheer chance. Like a professionally choreographed drama, all actors, actions, movements, and scenes were carefully chosen and divinely orchestrated.

The date and time of the Nazarene's birth, life, and death were set from eternity past, yet coming to pass in time. For that reason, the Nazarene frequently said, "My hour has not yet come" (John 2:4). By that He meant His appointed time, the time set by the Father. The apostle Paul said, "But when the fullness of time had come, God sent forth his Son, born of a woman, born under the law, to redeem those who were under the law…" (Galatians 4: 4-5). God becoming incarnate in the person of Jesus Christ, for the redemption of humans, was well planned and divinely fine-tuned to the very hour. God knows and sets the end of time from the beginning. He knows what world powers would be governing the earth and the character of their leaders and how they would serve the divine purpose. Jeremiah prophesied of the massacre of the children of Bethlehem by King Herod, in his attempt to kill the Christ child (Jeremiah 31: 15; Matthew 2: 16-18).

God in His omniscience and foreknowledge knew the world powers and leaders and what role they would play in His plan before they came to be. The book of Daniel informs us of those world powers because they were prophetically revealed to him decades before they came into being (Daniel 2 and 7).

God allowed those governments to be in place to fulfill His divine purpose. Nothing was left to chance in relation to God's plan of redemption through the Nazarene.

The prophets of the Old Testament predicted the details of the Messiah's birth, life, death, and resurrection (Isaiah 7:14, 9: 6-7; Micah 5: 2). The very price, thirty pieces of silver, that Judas betrayed the Nazarene for was not by chance; it was prophesied (Zacheriah 11:12-13; Matthew 26:14-16).

The betrayal kiss, even though a common greeting of the time between friends, was foretold (Psalm 41: 9; Mark 14: 43-46). The Nazarene was betrayed with a friendly kiss, given by a member of His own ministry team. Satan entered Judas as they reclined for the Last Supper and moved him to get up and cut the betrayal deal (John 13:26-30; John 17:12). Jeremiah was right, "the heart [of man] is deceitful above all things and desperately wicked..." (Jeremiah 17:9 NKJV). Each of us has a heart, we need to keep with all diligence.

The only material thing of value the Nazarene had was His robe or tunic, a long sleeve garment that reached down to the ankle and worn with a mantle. The garment was seamless; it required expert weaving skills to make, thus, more expensive. The high priest wore such garment.[1] Because of its value, the soldiers did not want to destroy it; they had a game a chance to determine who would own it. Even this was long foretold (Psalm 22: 18; Matthew 23: 35).

No, He was not crucified naked as some would have us believe; that was against Jewish law. He had a loincloth on, akin to what we would call underwear.[2]

Additionally, the Prophet Isaiah (53) gives us details about the Missiah's life: His humble upbringing, His trials before the authorities, the physical abuse He would suffer, the redemptive purpose of His death, He being assigned a grave with the wicked, yet buried in a rich man's tomb.

The soldiers would have buried the Him with the other criminals in the assigned grave, but Joseph of Arimathea, a rich man, stepped forward, claimed the body and buried it in a tomb he prepared for himself (John 19: 38-42).

The Nazarene was hung on the middle gallows, but even that was not coincidental. On the one hand, the religious elite wanted to disgrace Him not only by crucifixion but placing Him in the middle as the worst of the three criminals. But as you will see, even that was a divine orchestration.

The Roman soldiers who assigned the gallows to each of the three men would have had no preference for one over the other. To them, three criminals were going to die as usual, and they would be equally dead on anyone of the three gallows. They were just following orders. But that position was no accident; it was intended to show His as the worst.

Later that day, the head soldier, a centurion, would come to understand that this execution would be different from all the others he had experienced in his career. He had never seen a criminal behave with that level of self-control and dignity before. Nor had he ever witnessed such cosmic disturbance at any prior execution.

The midday became dark as a thousand midnights as the sun hid itself, the ground shook beneath his feet, bolts of lightning parted the sky and split rocks and rolled them out of their places, graves burst opened, the giant curtain in the temple ripped from top to bottom—shaken to the core of his being, the centurion cried out, "Truly, this was the Son of God!" (Matthew 27: 50-54; Luke 23: 44-47 ESV).

It is self-evident that this execution, though done by the conniving minds and wicked hands of men, was divinely choreographed. The hand of the Almighty was in every scene, every movement, and every utterance of this drama.

So, brutal men hardened by war and cruelty became tender and emotional, some for a moment, others would never be the same again. The crowd beholding the spectacle, shaken by what they had seen and heard, beat their breasts and went home (Luke (24: 48-49). The events of Golgotha was forever made indelible in their minds.

The Unmoved Religious Elite

Despite the obvious hand of God in all the happenings involving the Nazarene's life, and despite the revelation of Scripture that this person could very well be the long-expected Missiah for the redemption Israel and the world, the religious elite were unmoved, unconvinced, or just did not care who He was.

He was a threat to their comfortable lifestyle, and they wanted Him dead by all necessary means. And nothing was going to stand in their way to achieve that end. But they must do it cleverly so as not to arouse the common people with whom the Nazarene was popular.

Therefore, in as much as the Sanhedrin charged Him with blasphemy and could have stoned Him to death as they usually do with blasphemers, they knew the common people would not go with that, for they knew all along the hatred the religious elite was nursing against the Nazarene.

They were just waiting for the opportune time to execute their wicked plan. If they can charge Him with sedition against the Roman State, then they could have the Romans execute Him. The common people did not have the resources to successfully revolt against the Romans, their mighty military would crush any uprising. That was the plan!

The religious elites set out to use the mouth and message of the Nazarene to convict Him (Matthew 26:57-68). The Nazarene's mission and message was about the kingdom of God. He sees Himself as the Son of God and King over that kingdom. No king can rule Israel without first overthrowing the Roman government; His enemies knew.

That was the line of reasoning or talking-point Caiaphas, and his cronies used against Jesus, and they pushed hard to advance it to the intimidation of Pilate, the Roman governor. They knew Pilate was a political operative who would not stand to lose his position over this itinerant preacher from the peasant village of Nazareth. As expected, the governor capitulated, giving Caiaphas what he wanted.

So, on the one hand, we have religious conspiracy by a powerful elite to put an innocent man to death. And on the other hand, there is the compromise to push through the execution for political expediency on the part of the Roman governor, Pilate (John 18: 28-40).

The religious elites who were the Jewish ruling class, were all represented on the mighty Sanhedrin. There were three religious factions comprising Judaism at the time: the Pharisees, the Scribes, and the Sadducees. Caiaphas, the high priest, was the chairperson of this almost omnipotent council of 71 men with life and death powers over Jewish life. Except for two or three secret followers of the Nazarene, they all wanted Jesus dead in short order.

And they could have had Him stoned to death on the trumped-up charge of blasphemy, but the Nazarene was too popular with the common people to go that route. They would have had a riot on their hands that would attract the Roman military. Thus, killing the Nazarene themselves would have been counter-productive; they would have won the battle, but lost the war. They would have ended up in a more precarious place. There must be a better way, they thought, to protect ourselves and at the same time get rid of the Nazarene, this trouble-maker.

These lettered men of means, armed with political wizardry and with murderous hearts, piously camouflaged behind religious vestment, plotted the murder of an innocent man, the Nazarene.

They had to come up with another scheme, one to charge the Nazarene with crime against the Roman State and force the Roman governor to put Him on trial. The governor had to; he was the law enforcement officer of Caesar's government.

The governor asked them what the charge was. They said the Nazarene claimed to be King of the Jews but there is only one king and that is Caesar. The governor knew this was a political curved ball they threw at him, and he thought he caught it successfully. But did he?

The governor set out to try the Nazarene. "King of the Jews, so you are a king? the governor asked him. The Nazarene answered, yes, but my kingdom is not of this world, otherwise my servants would fight. With this questioning the governor concluded this man was no threat to Caesar's government; He was innocent of the charge. The governor was ready to set him free. But the crowd inspired by the high priest Caiaphas vehemently objected to His release (John 18: 33-38).

The governor then offered a compromise. Since it is Passover and it is customary to release a prisoner this time of the year, we will release the Nazarene. But again, Caiaphas and the mob he commanded objected, demanding the release of the notorious criminal named,

Barabbas and the execution of the Nazarene (John 18: 29-19:1-6). The governor then responded, "You take him and crucify him. As for me, I find no basis for a charge against him" (verse 6).

The governor continued to work for the release of the Nazarene until the high priest Caiaphas threw him a political hand grenade. He said, "this man claims to be a king, but we have no king but Caesar. If you let this man go, you are not Ceasar's friend. In other words, we will have Rome to recall you. With this the governor capitulated and handed over the Nazarene to be executed (John 19:7-16).

The Roman governor had an innocent man murdered to satisfy their ego and preserve their positions of influence. Yes, Caiaphas got what he worked so hard to achieve, the murder of the Nazarene. Yes, and that is how it was!

But wait, there is another side or hand to this intriguing story, and it is the hand of the divine earlier spoken about. The Nazarene's life was a sacrifice offered by the Almighty, not only for the murderers themselves but for all humankind. Speaking of the Nazarene, Isaiah gives us this prophetic, intelligence report:

> Surely, he took our pain and bore our suffering, yet we consider him punished by God, stricken by him, and afflicted. But he was pierced for our transgressions, he was crushed for our iniquities; the punishment that brought us peace was on him, and by his wounds we are healed. (Isaiah 53: 4-5)

The religious elites were not ignorant men, they had the holy Scriptures and were able to use it to tell king Herod the exact identity of the Nazarene: where He would be born, His ancestral lineage, and His mission (Matthew 2:1-12). They knew that the hand of God had guided the nation from its very beginning, calling, anointing, and commissioning prophets, priests, and kings (Genesis 12:1-9; Exodus 3).

The hand of God was evident in the Nazarene's life, mission, message, and ministry in miraculous acts of healing and wonders. Yet, the religious elites failed to see and acknowledge the presence of God in these wonders. They were spiritually blind or willfully ignorant or both.

We know from Scripture that there were at least two men of the religious elite who had a seat on Sanhedrin who were secret followers of Jesus. And they disagreed with their colleagues concerning the Nazarene. One was Nicodemus; the other Joseph of Arimathea (John 3:1-21, 19:38-42). They emerged from the shadows to claim the body of the Nazarene and gave it a decent burial. Even this detail the Prophet Isaiah spoke of 700 years earlier (Isaiah 53: 9).

Before we conclude this chapter, we will further reveal the hand of the divine by considering two other issues: 1) the gallows on which the Nazarene was executed, and 2) those who were executed with Him that fateful day.

The Gallows of the Nazarene

The Nazarene was strategically placed on the center gallows and two thieves, one on the right and the other on the left of him (Matthew 27: 38; Luke 23:32-33). To the soldiers carrying out the execution orders, the placement of one thief had no significance over the other. These were three criminals dying; and routine for soldiers. They just wanted to get it done and over with.

But in the divine economy, there was nothing routine about the transactions of this day. Every move was sacred, meaningful, and most significant. The Nazarie's death is the second great work of God Almighty. The first is the creation of the Universe, the second is the redemption of humankind, taking place on the center gallows (John 3: 14-18). It was a sacrifice offered to God for humankind (John 3: 16; Hebrews 10; 12-13).

Some will ask, what is the significance of the Nazarene being placed on the center gallows? This question is best answered by another question, what would two dying criminals need most? The answer is forgiveness and salvation. Who has what they need?

The man on the middle gallows of course. And because He is in the middle that gives Him equal access to each thief, and each thief equal access to Him. God is ensuring that all humankind, nations, peoples, cultures, and languages have access to Him (Matthew 28: 19-20). The Savior on the center gallows illustrates that.

But note the irony—some people, even though the Savior is close to them—they will not recognize Him, to take advantage of the free gift of salvation (John 3:16; Roman 6: 23). That fact is illustrated with what happened to these two men who had equal access to the Nazarene that fateful day.

Lefthand and Right-hand Thief

One thief on the lefthand side of the Nazarene and the other on His right; this is not without signification. From now on they will be referred to as such: the left-hand thief, and the right-hand thief. Again, the position each gallows occupied was not accidental or coincidence.

As the gripping crowd helplessly gazed in silence, the Nazarene breached the silence: "Mother behold thy son, son behold thy mother," He said (John 19: 26-27). The normal reaction of someone dying is to call for their mother, the one who brought him into this world. Perhaps she can help as he now makes his exit from it.

But not so with the Nazarene, He was not calling for help from His mother. He was telling His disciple John to take care of His mother. This is what He was saying, "Mother, John is now your son, John my mother is now your mother. Take care of her now because I am leaving." John understood the message and did exactly what was requested of him (John 19: 25-27).

Mary at this time was a widow and had little to no means of support but a good son would honor his mother by making some arrangements for her support.

If the two thieves were crying out for their mother, we do not know, there is no record of it. Jesus had family, friends, and supporters at the cross. Those who could do something did; they claimed the body and gave it a proper, decent, and dignified burial (Matthew 27:57-61; John 19:

38--42). But even this act of a rich man claiming the body of the Nazarene and laying it to rest in the tomb he prepared for himself was not coincidental; it was prophesied 700 years before by the prophet Isaiah (53: 9).

Conclusion

This chapter lays out the *grand concourse* of the man placed on the middle gallows. I want you to see that there was nothing accidental or coincidental about His death.

Every detail of the Nazarene's life was divinely orchestrated and prophetically forecast in the Hebrew Bible, our Old Testament. God wanted us to know that a Savior who is Christ the Lord was coming. His arrival would be a rescue mission, to seek and to save lost humanity and to give them a hope and a future (John 3:16).

Be especially keen now as we dive into this unfolding, redemptive drama with the man on the middle gallows. The best of men dying with the worst of men flanked on each side is perhaps, the most profound and compelling story of human history.

CHAPTER 2

THE TWO THIEVES

Their Unknown Biographies

The biographies of these two men are unknown to history; they remain nameless, only identified by their occupation as "two thieves" (Matthew 27:38; Mark 15:27). This may have been done by design, as part of the punishment, to prevent them gaining notoriety from their crimes. In this way they remain forever infamous to deter copycat revolutionaries.

Another reason for them being nameless is to protect innocent family members from further reprisal and perpetual public shame. But for sure if they did not have wives and children, they had parents and perhaps siblings as any normal, law-abiding family. Since the Nazarene's mother, a few followers, and close friends were there in the crowd to support him; chances are the mothers of the thieves, if no one else, would be huddling in the crowd weeping as the custom was (Luke 23: 27-28).

Furthermore, bear in mind that the two thieves were bearers of the divine image like you and me. They were no greater criminals that those white-collar elite who presided over the Sanhedrin's kangaroo trial of the Nazarene and condemned Him to death for blasphemy under the cover of dark. The process has all the markings of a cover-up. But why would these highly esteemed men do such a ghastly thing? The answer is clear in all four gospels.

The Nazarene was too popular to arrest, try, and kill Him in broad daylight. It was a night trial which was forbidden by their own law (Matthew 25:31-74). The civil trial started early in the morning (Matthew 27:1).

Later, the members of the Sanhedrin continued their mockery by railing on the Roman governor to release a murderer named Barabbas and execute the Nazarene who was innocent (Luke 23:13-25). They did this ghastly thing because they were in a place of power and privilege and wanted to humiliate the Nazarene in the worse way.[1]

The two thieves are remembered by history only because they were executed with the man on the middle gallows, the man who divides history into AD and BC. Their encounter with the Nazarene changed everything. Yes, they were still executed, but their story is memorialized with the Nazarene's story forever in history.

The focus of this chapter is on these two men who cross path with that lowly figure on the middle gallows; the man from the peasant village of Nazareth. Their encounter with Him was not happenstance, accident or coincidence; it was a divine setup, as we have already seen and will continue to see as the drama unfolds.

The two partners in crime that the biblical text left nameless were no ordinary, petty thieves. The Pulpit Commentary asserts that they were part of the Barabbas insurrectionist movement (Luke 23:32).[2] They were what some today would call freedom fighters or revolutionaries, but others would flag as terrorists. Those doing the fight for freedom and justice see themselves as freedom fighters, while others tend to see them as terrorists. One man's meat is sometimes another man's poison.

They are called thieves, but other crimes are connected to what they were commonly known for, perhaps murder, or attempted murder of government officials and workers such as soldiers, and tax-collectors. Any representative of the oppressive Roman State was a welcome target. The fact that these men were given the ultimate punishment of public execution suggest that they were a threat to the Roman State. That would qualify them not just for a prison term but death.

There were always uprisings this time of the year by trouble-makers, Barabbas-type revolutionaries, attempting to throw off oppression of the occupying State as Moses did to a former empire that enslaved the Israelites. It was Passover season and messianic, liberation fervor would be high in the air.

There was high expectation for the appearance of the Jewish Messiah to end tyranny and restore Israel to the glory days of King David and Solomon. To that end Barabbas-type revolutionaries were plentiful to fill that void, in case the Messiah did not appear.

The Gallows of the Thieves

All four Gospels speak of the two thieves executed with Yeshua (Jesus), one on the left and the other on the right. It is shown in the previous chapter that there was nothing accidental or coincidental in the Nazarene's life, everything was divinely orchestrated. With that in mind, we must conclude that the two thieves were also strategically positioned, intentionally by humans and by heaven. By humans: to humiliate, and by heaven to fulfill the Scriptures.

The gallows of the penitent thief on the right hand of the Nazarene, and the gallows of the unrepentant thief on the left of the Nazarene. Why? The religious elite intended the focus to be on the Nazarene as the lead criminal; those on His side as supporters of the same cause against the State.

We already stated the reason the Nazarene was placed by heaven on the center gallows. The Nazarene is a sacrifice being offered to God; that gallows is akin to an altar (John 3: 16). What the two thieves needed most was forgiveness and salvation. With the Nazarene in the center, He had equal access to the two thieves, and they had equal access to Him. But there is something else of significance here.

In the economy of God, the right hand is the position of favor. This is reflected in some ancient cultures and in numerous biblical texts in both Old and New testaments. The right hand is used figuratively in scripture to symbolize the place of favor, honor, power, authority, and protection. A person could be given one or more of these privileges.

In Exodus 15, the Israelites celebrated the drowning of Pharoh's army in the Red Sea by singing a song of Moses in praise to God. Verse six of that song says, "Your right hand, LORD, was majestic in power. Your right hand, LORD, shattered the enemy" (Exodus 15:6).

King David prayed, "Show me the wonders of your great love, you who save by your right hand those who take refuge in you from their foes" (Psalm 17:7). Because God favor His people, He fought their battles, pushed down their enemies and planted them in the land of Canaan as their inheritance. The Psalmist expresses it this way:

> We have heard with our ears, O God, our ancestors have told us what you did in their day, in days long ago. With your hand you drove out the nations and planted our ancestors; you crushed the peoples and made our ancestors flourish. It was not by their sword that they won the land, nor did their arm bring them victory; it was your right hand, your arm, and the light of your face, for you loved them. (Psalm 44:1-3)

The preceding Psalm speaks of God's right hand, the place of favor, protection and power. It speaks of God's arm; that refers to His strength. The strength of the hand is in the arm. The arm extends the reach of the hand. We speak of the long arm of the law.

Finally, the Psalm speaks of the love of God for His people, and the light of His countenance, which again is a reference to walking in the love and favor of God.

The right hand in scripture also speaks of God's support. The Psalmist declares, "I am always with you; you hold me by my right hand" (Psalm 73: 23); the Prophet Isaiah makes the same declaration in Isaiah (41: 13-14).

The right hand signifies favor and blessing. Joseph positioned his first-born son, Ephraim, at Jacob's right hand, and Manasseh on Jacob's left for the blessing. But Jacob crossed his hand to put his right hand on Manasseh who was standing on his left. Joseph thought his father made a mistake and attempted to uncross his hand. But Jacob refused, asserting that both boys will receive a blessing and will be great, but the younger boy on whom he placed his right hand will be greater (Genesis 48:12-16).

The right hand is not only the place of favor but the place of honor. In 2 King 2:19, Bathsheba went to the palace to speak with the young king Solomon. As she walked in "the king stood up to meet her and bowed down to her...." Solomon then "had a throne brought for the king's mother, and she sat at his right hand."

Jesus at His religious trial before the Sanhedrin was interrogated by the high priest. "Are you the Messiah, the Son of the Blessed One? the high priest asked. Jesus responded, I am, and you will see the Son of Man sitting at the right hand of the Mighty One and coming on the clouds of heaven" (Mark 14:61-62). The high priest was flabbergasted at this answer to the point of rending his clothes. He ended the questioning and immediately charged Jesus with blasphemy and condemned Him to death (Mark 14: 63-65).

But upon His ascension, Jesus was indeed exalted to right hand of God, the Father (Philippians 2: 5-11; Hebrews 1: 3-4). Stephen, a man full of the Holy Spirit, the first martyr of the Church, when stoned to death by religious zealots gave this testimony, "Look...I see heaven open and the Son of Man standing at the right hand of God" (Acts 7:55-56).

Since the life and death of the Nazarene was divinely choreographed, we assert that everything that happened in connection with or to Him had a purpose. All participants were strategically placed and played their part as a well conducted orchestra. Most did so unwittingly.

We will not make a doctrine out of it, but the penitent thief had to be the one situated to the right hand of the Nazarene and the unrepentant thief to His left. The righthand is the place of favor, the lefthand the place of judgment and condemnation (Matthew 24:31-44).

That does not mean both men could not have received salvation. One being on the left was not causative; his wicked heart was the problem. So, don't say, it is because he was on the left; that would be absurd! We do not even know that for sure. Salvation is not forced on anyone; it is the gift of God, freely given with no strings attached. But you must repent and receive it; he did not (John 3:16; Romans 6:23).

Therefore, let no one say the thief on the left of the Nazarene was destined for hell because he was on the left. Such a conclusion would be biblically and theologically absurd. Jesus forgave his executioners because they acted ignorantly and were soldiers following orders. He would have forgiven Judas, but he hung himself instead of repenting and seeking forgiveness. Jesus forgave Peter and restored him to ministry (John 21).

Criminal Facing Criminal

The two thieves were facing death for their crimes, and they did not deny that they were guilty as charged. They knew in advance that if they were caught, their lives would end as they were now ending, lights out on Roman gallows.

During the early hours of the execution process, while their bodies were still strong and minds sharp, they could mentally review the life they lived and show remorse or give their final protest against what they considered an unjust system.

But their individual gallows were not placed beside each other; there was the third gallows between them. Who is this man on the middle gallows blocking our limited line of sight and communication, they perhaps wondered.

Finally, they recognized the man on the center gallows. He is the itinerant preacher and healer from the peasant village of Nazareth who claimed to be Messiah and Son of God. He is the non-violent do-gooder who believed His approach would change things. But here he is dying with us. How in heaven did he end up with us on Roman gallows, they reasoned. He used to be called king of the Jews; I knew that would have gotten Him in trouble but not being publicly executed like us. One or both thieves could have had such line of reasoning. We don't know.

By this time, they heard the chant from the mocking crowd, if you be the Son of God, come down from the cross and save yourself. At first both thieves joined with the crowd mocking Jesus. Yes, if you are the son of God, come down from the gallows, save yourself and us (Matthew 27:39-44;Mark 15:32).

But after a while the thief on the righthand of Jesus stopped his mocking. He observed the dignity with which Jesus comport himself, even gracious enough to forgive His executioners. Perhaps, He is whom He claims to be, the King of the Jews, the Son of God. This thief changed his mind about this man on the middle gallows dying beside him. He is innocent, he concluded. But I am guilty as charged, he muttered. He repented!

But his companion in crime on the other side, left of the Nazarene was still casting insults, and railing at the Nazarene with the crowd saying, "Aren't you the Messiah? Save yourself and us! (Luke 23:39 NIV). But the thief to the right of Jesus rebuked his companion saying, "Don't you fear God, since you are under the same sentence? We are punished justly, for we are getting what our deeds deserve, but this man has done nothing wrong" (Luke 23: 40-41). He defended the Nazarene!

Having confessed publicly, taking responsibility for his crime, he rebuked his partner in crime for not discerning the difference between their life of crime and the life of the man on the middle gallows. His ungodly soul tie with his partner in crime was finally broken. And with that, he turned his attention to the Nazarene and said, "Remember me when you come into your kingdom." Note he did not say, remember us because he was not speaking for the other thief. He said, "Remember me." The reply to his request was immediate, "Truly I tell you, today you will be with me in paradise" (Luke 23: 42-43 NIV).

It was as if both men came to a fork in the road they were traveling, and each took a different turn leading to different eternal destinations. The penitent thief made a conscious decision to go his own way, leaving his cursing companion to make his own decision. This is an intersection in life that all of us will arrive at one time or another, during the years of our pilgrimage. Let's explore this all-important contrast some more.

The Obvious Contrast

Note the contrast between these two men. The one on the righthand side of the Nazarene, the penitent thief, used his dying breath to make amends: he took responsibility for his crime, he said the penalty received was just. He rebuked his companion, he defended the innocence of the Nazarene, he believed the claims of the Nazarene to be the King of the Jews, the Messiah, the Son of God who heads up a kingdom. He then asked for the Nazarene's help and received it. With that act of contrition, he changed destination hell to destination paradise. His is the miraculous turn-around that often happen when a sincere and penitent sinner encounters the Lord Jesus Christ.

With the cross of the Christ, every person arrives at an intersection and must make a destination choice. It is for this reason Billy Graham named his broadcast, the Hour of Decision. The cross also has a way of separating chief friends with opposite values and moral convictions. Sometimes, it separates family members who want to go their own way.

The thief to the left-hand side of the Nazarene had the same opportunity to change as his repentant friend, but he chose not to. He used his last breath to rail on the Savior. He failed to discern the difference between his life of crime and the life of the Son of God. The irony is—they were both the same physical distance from the Nazarene, but one failed to see himself and he failed to see the Savior for who He was.

He failed to repent, and therefore, continued to a destination from which his partner in crime had made a dramatic turn-around. It's a pity he did not come along; he was so close yet so far. He was close as John 3: 16.

The unbelieving thief on the left, was like many of his fellow Jews who had the revelation of God's Word in hand for decades but failed to recognize Him. The Jews encountered the Christ face to face again and again but remain blind and tone-deaf to His identity to this day as the unrepentant thief was. The god of this world (Satan) has blinded the eyes and minds of those who do not believe (2 Corinthians 4: 4-6; John 3:16-18).

Some suggest that—for the penitent thief to draw the conclusion of Jesus' innocence, suggest some knowledge of Jesus' ministry and message about the kingdom of God. That is possible. But it would also be possible that his partner in crime possessed the same knowledge. But he could not see the logic of the Nazarene having the same fate as two common thieves, unless He was the imposter they said He was. With that conclusion, he continued with the crowd to throw provocative insults at Jesus, even when cautioned by his partner.

There were those who made sport of Jesus on the premise that if they could make Him angry enough, he would work His magic to save himself. And that would be the proof of His claim to kingship and divinity that they could accept.

But Jesus could not be provoked to yield to such Satanic stunt to prove His legitimacy. Satan tried all that trick at the beginning of Jesus' ministry and Jesus rebuked him three times (Matthew 4:1-11). Later, Jesus told the Jews who demanded miraculous proof of His Messiahship and divinity for them to believe Him—that the only miraculous sign they would get is His resurrection. He told them that as Jonah was in the belly of the big fish three days and three nights, so will the Son of Man be in the heart of the earth three day and three nights (Matthew 12: 38-40; Luke 11: 29-32). Why this sign only? Because it is the only miracle Satan cannot duplicate.

Judas, whom Jesus handpicked to be part of His ministry team, had come to a similar conclusion that when backed into a corner, the Nazarene always find a way out. Judas wanted to throw off the Roman yoke of oppression so urgently—that He quietly disapproved of Jesus' non-violent method. But if I force His hand, Judas reasoned, the Nazarene will act when He finds Himself between the proverbial rock and a hard place. Judas watched Him miraculously escape death several times before. He will do it again, Judas thought.

With this faulty conclusion, Judas pulled back from the Last Supper table under the cover of dark to cut the betrayal deal with the Jewish religious authorities for thirty pieces of silver. They were most delighted to have this inside man on Jesus' ministry team. Now they can know His whereabouts anytime of the day.

When Judas discovered that he was wrong, that his little scheme did not work, rather than repent and ask for forgiveness, he hung himself. What caused him to do that? Shame and a sense of hopelessness. But he was not hopeless. He was in crisis mode and not thinking irrationally. He hung himself, and not even that Judas did successfully, because the rope gave way, and he fell in a rocky gorge below and his intestines spilled all over the place (Matthew 27: 1-5; Act 1: 12-20).

What does Judas and the unrepentant thief have in common? On the surface it looks like they had nothing in common but look again and you will see several parallel lines.

For one, they were both wrong about the Nazarene. Second, they both wanted the same thing, the revolutionary overthrow of the oppressive Roman State and the restoration of Israel's golden years. They were both Barabbas sympathizers. Third, in a sense, they were both physically close to the Nazarene, though not equally so. How so?

Judas was part of the Nazarene's ministry team and was involved with the Nazarene for three years. The two thieves were only close to Nazarene for the hours spent beside Him on the gallows. The unrepentant thief used those hours to mock the Nazarene. He joined the crowd to chant, "If you are the Son of God come down from the cross, save yourself and us. In other words, now that your back is between a rock and a hard place, use your magic to show who you are. That was Judas' motivation. And where did it come from?

Judas was inspired by Satan. Satan tempted the Nazarene in the desert to use His powers to prove that He is the Son of God. He prodded the Nazarene to satisfy His hunger by turning stone into bread; to jump off the six-hundred-foot pinnacle of the temple into the rocky gorge below unharmed. That would prove who He was. Don't worry about jumping, the Scripture said angels will catch you, Satan said to Jesus (Matthew 4: 1-11).

Satan was very much present on Golgotha that Spring Day, working overtime to prevent the Nazarene from fulfilling His God-assigned mission. Satan thought he won the fight with the execution of the Nazarene, but the resurrection proved him wrong. The lifting up of the Nazarene was the casting down of Satan. The Nazarene crushed the serpent's head, and the serpent bruised His heel (Genesis 3:14-15).

Conclusion

On the one hand, the execution of the Nazarene on Golgotha that awful Spring Day was the work of wicked men inspired by Satan. Yet on the other hand, it was the unfolding drama of the mighty redemptive work of God for the salvation of humankind.

We are witnessing the drama of redemption, divinely choreographed and unfolding in living color. On the one hand, we see God the Father, God the Son, and God the

Holy Spirit, all three persons of the blessed Holy Trinity working as one, to put into effect God's great work of redemption as they worked together to put into effect their great work of creation. On the other hand, we see Satan and his human cohorts at work trying to frustrate the process.

Yet, redemption is a rescue mission for humans only. But not all humans will accept this generous offer from God. It will be close to them as the Nazarene was to the two thieves. Some will recognize Him and be saved, but others will not and be lost (John 3: 16).

The Nazarene's own people condemned Him to death and to prevent an uprising from the common people, they prevailed against the Roman governor to carry out their dirty work. But what they meant for evil God used for the redemption of humankind. It recalls the story of Joseph.

Joseph said to his wicked brothers who sold him into slavery, "You meant it for evil; but God meant it for good" (Genesis 50: 20). Jesus said, No man takes my life from me, I have power to lay it down, and power to pick it up again (John 10: 18). Every movement of this drama was beautifully choreographed by the Almighty Himself (Isaiah 53; Galatians 4: 4).

CHAPTER 3

THE NAZARENE'S RESPONSE TO A THIEF

Three dying men: one cussing, the other repenting, the other listening. The penitent thief having recognized the identity of the man beside him on the middle gallows said, "Jesus, remember me, when you come into your kingdom." "Truly I tell you, today you will be with me in paradise," the Nazarene responded (Luke 23:39-43). Indeed, he was listening and heard both the cussing from one thief and the cry for help coming from the other. It is important to note that the penitent thief addressed the Nazarene by name.

Both the request and the response raise several questions such as: how well did the thief know the Nazarene to make such a request? Where is Paradise, did they go to Paradise that day? What was the mission to Paradise all about? Where is Paradise today? This chapter seeks to explore and answer these questions.

Remember Me

The repentant thief asked to be remembered, a sobering and thoughtful request indeed. No well thinking person wants to be forgotten; we all want to be remembered. We will do everything in our power to survive, but if we cannot, at least, we want it memorialized that we were here. Sometimes we want it done in a certain way, but the thief did not specify. He perhaps thought, "after all I am just a thief, to be remembered is enough to ask."

With prior knowledge of His own death, the Nazarene Himself made a similar request of His disciples when He celebrated the Passover and instituted the Last Supper with them. This was the Thursday evening before he was arrested. He instructed them to celebrate this new feast of bread and wine in remembrance of Him. He said, "This do in remembrance of me" (Luke 22:17-20).

Note how the Nazarene wanted to be remembered— not by naming a building or street or park after Him. But to have this simple love feast of breaking bread and sharing a cup of wine. This act celebrates His redemptive work on the cross until He comes again. "In Remembrance of Me" is engraved on communion tables in churches everywhere.

But as you have already seen, the celebration of this love feast in remembrance of the Nazarene has a deeper meaning than the simple recall of His name. It is a celebration of His redemptive work on the gallows that day. It ushered in a completely new era for all humankind. An era of redemption, forgiveness, and hope beyond death.

Again, on the Thursday night before His death, the Nazarene celebrated the Passover feast and instituted the Lord's Supper. The Passover was in remembrance of the Israelite's deliverance from the tyranny of an earlier empire (Egypt) under the leadership of Moses.

The first Passover lamb was eaten on the night of their deliverance, and the blood of that lamb was applied to the doorpost of each Israelite's house before the death angel passed through the land of Egypt (Exodus 12:1-11).

Every house without the protection of lamb's blood had a death that night. But the Israelites had no death because the death angel passed over their houses. As of that night the Passover is celebrated yearly in remembrance of God's intervention for His people (Exodus 12; Psalm 44).

But the Passover not only looks back to that night of Israel's deliverance; it also looks forward to Calvary, where the true Lamb of God would be offered up as a sacrifice to God for the redemption of all humankind, including thieves and executioners alike (John 3:14-18). The Nazarene knew all that and welcomed the request of the thief on that fateful day without hesitation.

The thief did not know it then, but his request to be remembered was made in the same context in which we now remember the Nazarene at the communion table Sunday after Sunday. We are celebrating His redemptive work on the gallows He submitted Himself willingly that day. It is in this context also we remember the thief. This thief can now turn to the Nazarene and say, "Sir, it was an honor dying with you." The Nazarene can respond, "It was a pleasure dying for you."

The thief's request was profound, it moves us to ask, how much did he know of the Nazarene to make such a sobering request? Frankly, this question was partly addressed in chapter two. We do not know how much he knew of Jesus before. It is very possible he was acquainted with the Nazarene's ministry. Whether that be the case are not—he had divine help from above.

Because this thief was truly penitent, the Holy Spirit revealed the identity of the Christ to him. This is the Messiah, the Son of God, the head of a kingdom. No one can know that Jesus is the Son of God unless it is revealed to him or her by heaven (Matthew 16: 13-19).

When You Come into Your Kingdom

The penitent thief is not asking to be rescued from the pain of execution or death; he had already concluded that he and his partner in crime were getting their just due for the crimes they committed. For that reason, he rebuked his companion to stop hurling insults at the Nazarene, who in his judgment was innocent of any crime. What a revelation!

But even more awesome, this thief understands the Nazarene to be a King who will come to head up a kingdom in the future. "Remember me when you come into your kingdom," he said. It is a line Jesus taught His disciples, "When you pray...pray thy kingdom come, thy will be done on earth as it is in heaven" (Matthew 6: 9).

If the other thief had listened to the rebuke of this thief and pay close attention to the Nazarene, he too could have seen that he was in the company of the Son of God and could have cried out for help as well. All three of them could have gone to Paradise that day.

But his wicked heart and loose lips blinded him from discerning with the other thief whose company he was in. "The god of this world has blinded the minds of them that believe not, less the light of the glorious gospel of Christ who is the image of God should shine unto them," says the apostle Paul (2 Corinthians 4: 4 KJV).

Two men the same distance from the Son of God but they saw Him differently. One used his mouth to seal his fate to hell, while the other used his mouth to cancel his ticket to the same place. Indeed, "the heart is deceitful above all things and desperately wicked" and "the tongue has the power of life and death"(Jer.17: 9; Proverbs 18: 21).

How appropriate are the words: "For with the heart man believe unto righteousness, and with the mouth confession is made unto salvation" (Romans 9:10). The penitent thief recognized the Messiah, the King of Glory, the one who is the head of a kingdom, and asked for help and received it. This help was available to everyone in the crowd that day.

The other thief saw a criminal like himself and cursed him. This dual vision of the Nazarene runs through all of life, even in the same family. Some recognize Him as the Savior and Lord, others don't. It divides the world into believers and unbelievers. The penitent thief received an immediate response to his request.

The Nazarene's Response

Like the last bite of a delicious steak, this is a moment worth savoring! Two men, same crime, same punishment, but their reaction to the man on the middle gallows made all the difference: one used his last breath to curse the Nazarene and the other to call on Him for help and received it. He is referred to as the penitent thief.

What did he ask for? Did he ask for a Houdini type miracle that both could escape off the gallows? Not at all! He asked to be remembered when the Nazarene returns to reign in His kingdom. This is an insightful request. Why so?

If the Nazarene is coming back to reign as the head of a kingdom, He must be able to conquer death. If the dying thief knew all that then and there, he also knew that the Nazarene was the Son of God. That is revelation knowledge from heaven as it was earlier given to Peter (Matthew 16: 13-17).

The response to the thief's request to be remembered was immediate. No sinner's prayer, no baptism, but a blessed assurance of Paradise was given. "Today, you will be with me in paradise" was the response the Nazarene gave him. It signals to all of us that "Everyone who calls upon the name of the Lord will be saved" (Roman 10: 13). "For [indeed], the Son of Man came to seek and to save that which was lost."

This thief received salvation that day because he had an encounter with the Savior and repented. He changed his mind about the man on the center gallows and called upon Him for help. This is exactly what all of us are asked to do to secure our own salvation to Paradise. To repent and receive Salvation, we must do the same (John 3:16).

The Response to You

What is the Nazarene saying to you today? Are you nailed to your personal gallows and cannot free yourself? Are you crying out and is anyone hearing you? What is God doing on a cross beside a dying thief anyway?

This last question is the irony of the situation, because it shows that God is not distant from any of us. He is right there amid our human predicaments. He is suffering alongside the worst of us. And He is not suffering for Himself; He is suffering for us. "Surely he has borne our griefs and carried our sorrows…he was wounded for our transgressions; he was crushed for our iniquities…and with his stripes we are healed" (Isaiah 53: 4-5 ESV).

This is the profound mystery of the incarnation, God becoming man, and sharing our humanity. There is a popular song that summarizes it well: "When I got a glimpse of true love, it was hanging from an old rugged cross." This is the message of John 3:16 that even a small child should know from memory: "For God so love the world that he gave his one and only Son that whoever believes in him should not perish but have eternal life." Each one of us is included in this verse.

So, whether you are serving time unjustly behind bars for a crime you did not commit. Or you are fired from a job you gave twenty years of your life, just as you were about to retire and collect your pension. Or there is an inoperable cancer eating your body away. In all this we cry out, "God where are you?" He seems deaf to your cries and too distant to care. The irony is, He is right there beside you as He was beside those two thieves that fateful day.

Yes, He was right there in their midst; yet, only a few recognized Him, including a dying thief. The religious and political leaders failed to recognize Him. You are not alone in your predicament as you may feel and think. And if you are not careful you can become bitter like the unrepentant thief. And use your dying breath to curse God and become eternally lost as he did. Or you can be like the penitent thief. He embraced his suffering like the man on the middle gallows embraced His suffering to the point of saying a prayer forgiving his executioners (Luke 23:33-34).

That prayer moved the penitent thief to see that this man is innocent. He is exactly who He said He is—the Son of God, the King of Glory, the head of a kingdom. With that recognition, this thief cried out for mercy and received it. With that he changed his eternal destination. The things we suffer have the potential to make us or break us. But if we allow it, the grace of God is sufficient in any and every situation, even in our dying hour (2 Corinthians 12: 9).

There are some predicaments that God does not choose to deliver us from; He uses them to bring glory to Himself. Here is one such case. The disciples saw a man who was born blind, panhandling for a living by the roadside. They wanted to know why this man was in this predicament. So, they asked Jesus, "Who sinned, this man or his parents, that he was born blind?"

The popular culture of the time said that curse was a result of personal or ancestral sins. But Jesus said, "Neither this man nor his parents sinned, but that the works of God should be revealed in him." And with that He healed the man" (John 9:1-4 NKJV). Think of the relief, the deliverance that man and his parents experienced that day.

The story signals to us that some human predicaments are for God's glory and are intended for the greater good, to teach others near and far how God works. They are blessings to us and not a curse. But it is hard to see God in our personal predicaments when we are hurting.

Two thieves, dying beside each other with the Son of God, the Savior of humankind between them; one missed it, the other recognized the Christ and cried out for help. It is difficult to accept suffering as God's will but sometimes it is the instrument God uses to save us and bless others.

We all want to be delivered from our suffering, and there is nothing wrong with that. We would not be human if we did not want that. Even the Nazarene explored that option with His Father in Gethsemane. He prayed three times, "Father, if it is possible, let this cup pass from me." It was possible but it was not the Father's will, so He submitted His human will to the will of God and embraced the suffering (Matthew 26: 36-46).

Sometimes suffering and even dying is God's will, and He will not rescue us from it. Because there is a greater good to be accomplished with your suffering. The book of Job is the classic literature on human suffering, how God uses suffering for His own purpose and glory.

The penitent thief was not delivered from the gallows; he died that day. But he was delivered from something far worse than suffering and death. He was delivered from hell itself, and his experience serves as a teaching example of hope for all times.

What are the Other Lessons?

There are many lessons to extrapolate from the story of both thieves that died on the opposite side of the Nazarene that day. They may have been sentenced for the same crime, but each died a different death, and each went to different eternal destination.

One recognized the Savior, repented, and asked for mercy and received it. The other used his dying breath to curse the Savior and continued to his original destination.

We learn a little about the problem of suffering, that sometimes God uses it for a greater good and may not rescue us from our suffering or even death.

We learn a little about the sovereignty of God, that He works all things for His own purpose and glory.

We also learn that there is hope up to our dying hour, but wisdom dictates that it is not wise to delay calling upon the Savior to such late an hour.

CHAPTER 4

THE TRIP TO PARADISE

What is Paradise, and where is it? Paradise is a Persian word (*Pardes*) which means park or garden. It is not strange that a Persian word made its way into the Hebrew vocabulary because after Babylonian subjugation, the Hebrews came under Persian rule (Daniel 5: 24-30, 10: 1). The Hebrews used the word Paradise to signify a "pleasure garden like the Garden of Eden" and "the abode of the righteous after death."[1]

Even in our time, the Twenty-first Century, the Garden of Eden is referred to as the "Paradise Garden" and the Fall of man as *Paradise lost* as Dante's *Divine Comedy* so aptly portrays. With the expulsion of humans from the Paradise

Garden, high ranking angels were assigned to guard the tree of life, to prevent humans from returning to eat from the tree of life. And in so doing live forever in their sinful state (Genesis 3: 22-24). Since the Paradise Garden has disappeared from earth, we must conclude that God has relocated it, perhaps, subterranean or in the heavens.

Therefore, we must further conclude that when the Nazarene said to the penitent thief, "You will be with me in Paradise," they were positioned to go from their present location to another place: upward, downward, or outward. The weight of the evidence point sharply downward.

If the Hebrew Scripture is the inspired Word and Revelation of God, we must take what it says seriously. Jesus did! The Hebrew Scripture, theology, and tradition placed Paradise in or near Sheol. Sheol translates Hades in Geek. In Old Testament (OT) times, it was subterranean.

In the process of time, the word *Paradise* came to be used in three ways: 1) to refer to the original Garden of Eden, 2) to signify the abode of the righteous dead prior to their resurrection, and 3) the place of eternal abode for the righteous. It is not three different places but perhaps different levels of the same place. In Hebrew thought, when a person exits the body, he or she descends into Sheol.[2] Greeks would say, descend into Hades.

Again, Paradise was believed to be a section of Sheol or located in the vicinity of Sheol as a gated community would be separated from the larger township. Paradise was and is for righteous souls only. The OT points to the underworld or in another dimension or realm.

Jesus and the New Testament (NT) give us significant insight into this place called *Paradise*, its whereabouts, and what it is used for. But the teachings of Jesus on Paradise is not far from the Hebraic thought on the matter. Humanly, Jesus is of the Hebraic cultural lineage; His Bible was the Hebrew Scriptures (Luke 2:1-7; Luke 24:13-27).

In Hebrew thought and in the teachings of Jesus, Paradise appears to have been one compartment of Sheol. The other compartment is hell, but not the final help. We will identify five characteristics about Sheol and Paradise and answer them in one story that summarizes the teachings of Jesus on the subject.

First, to Jesus Paradise is the abode of the righteous dead before resurrection of the body. **Second**, Paradise was in the underworld or another dimension or realm.

Third, Sheol or Hades (the place of abode for departed souls) was divided into hell for the wicked dead (not the final hell), and Paradise for the righteous dead. Paradise was also referred to as Abraham's bosom.

Fourth, the souls in each compartment of Sheol could see each other but could not get to each other because of a great gulf separating the two places.

Fifth, the souls in each compartment of Sheol were alive and conscious; they had memories of the life lived in the physical body. Sheol is not the grave as some would have us believe; the story of Jesus puts that to rest.

Now, look for all five characteristics in the following story that summarizes the teachings of Jesus about Sheol, including Paradise. The story is told by Jesus Himself, it is not a parable; it is concerning two living persons and what happened to them after death:

> There was a rich man who was clothed in purple and fine linen and feasted sumptuously every day. And at his gate was laid a poor man named Lazarus, covered with sores, who desired to be fed with what fell from the rich man's table. Moreover, even the dogs came and licked his sores.
>
> The poor man died and was carried off by angels into Abraham's side. The rich man also died and was buried, and in Hades being tormented, he lifted up his eyes and saw Abraham far off and Lazarus at his side. And he called out, Father Abraham, have mercy on me, and send Lazarus to dip the end of his finger in water to cool my tongue, for I am in anguish in this flame.
>
> But Abraham said, Child, remember that in your lifetime received your good things, and Lazarus in like manner bad things; but now he is comforted here, and you are in anguish. And besides all this, between us and you a great chasm has been fixed, in order that those who would pass from here to you may not be able, and no one may cross from there to us.

And he said, "Then, I beg you, father, to send him to my father's house—for I have five brothers—so that he may warn them, lest they also come into this place of torment. But Abraham said, "They have Moses and the Prophets, let them hear them." And he said, "No father Abraham, but if someone goes to them from the dead, they will repent." He said to him, "If they do not hear Moses and the Prophets, neither will they be convinced if someone should rise from the dead." (Luke 16: 19-31 ESV).

So, the teachings of Jesus on Sheol or Hades is summarized in the preceding quotation, and it does not contradict Hebrew thought or teaching on the subject. To my understanding, therefore, Paradise was seen as a compartment of Sheol or situated in the same region.

It is fair to conclude that up to the time of Jesus' death, Paradise was believed to be in the underworld, or in another dimension or realm. It was accessible only by those who have died (Matthew 16:18).

The souls of the departed when to Sheol; the wicked were quartered in the place of torment, at times referred to as hell, but not the final hell. And the righteous souls were stationed in the pleasant compartment known as Paradise. Paradise, though a pleasant place, was not considered to be heaven. But the presence of God is there (Ps.139:7-8).

According to what Jesus said about the rich man and Lazarus, the poor beggar, Sheol is a place of conscious existence outside of the physical body. Those in one compartment could see and hear those in the other, but they could not get across to each other because of a great gulf fixed between them. Jesus said to the penitent thief on the cross, "Truly, I say unto you, today you will be with me in Paradise." Both men died that day and by extension went to Paradise. We have no reason to believe otherwise.

The righteous souls from Adam and Eve to the death of Jesus would have gone to Paradise, whereas the wicked would have gone to the compartment of Sheol, sometimes referred to as hell (not the final hell). The wicked thief who died the same day would also show up in Sheol, but not the Paradise section. Why Jesus had to personally visit this place known as Paradise? Let's explore this question.

War and Victory in Sheol

The war against Satan began in the heavens, fought on earth but did not end on the cross (Revelation 12; Matthew 4:1-11). Presumably, the fight continued fiercely in the underworld, that dimension called Sheol or Hades which can only be accessed out of the physical body. Death appears to be the gateway into Sheol (Matthew 16:18-19).

A war consists of more than one battle. Jesus wont the battle over Satan on the cross, but the war was not yet won. He won the victory as a man in the physical body against Satan. But His victory was not certified for the war was not over until His triumphant resurrection on Easter morning. It is like winning a Presidential election in the United States; that victory must be certified for the transfer of powers.

Did Satan accept the death of Christ on the cross as a victory for the Nazarene? The answer is no! Satan thought he won, that is why the *Resurrection of the Christ* is the decisive victory and public certification of who won this battle royal. It is the foundation of faith (1 Corinthian 15).

Therefore, the real war as a disembodied "spirit-being" was fought in the underworld in that place called, Sheol and Hades (1Peter 3:18-22). We are not seeking to establish a dogmatic theology on the matter, but scripture seems to point in this direction; therefore, we must give it serious consideration under the guidance of the blessed Holy Spirt. Jesus went to Paradise, why?

Satan did not accept the death of Christ on the cross as a decisive victory in favor of the Nazarene. Jesus had to personally visit Sheol to exercise Lordship in that domain by defeating Satan, taking away his authority for all times. If Satan had lordship as prince over the atmospheric heaven, there is no reason to believe that he did not exercise some control over the underworld (compare Isaiah 14:12-15; Revelation 17: 8).

Satan made a big mistake and that is possible because he is a finite creature. He thought he had finally succeeded killing Jesus on the cross. He had been trying to kill Jesus from birth (Matthew 2: 1-23). He also tried to bribe Jesus, buy Him off but Jesus refused him (Matthew 4:1-11).

Satan appears to have had big authority in Sheol, a place where he had his own in prison such as the rich man that was crying out to Lazarus for help, the rebellious souls of Noah's generation, and those destroyed in the fire of

Sodom and Gomorrah (Luke 16: 22-26; 1 Peter 3:18-20; Jude 6-7). Satan has legal authority over those who are under God's judgment and permanently so, if they die in their sinful condition without the Savior (John 3:18-21). We also know that God is present in Sheol and exercises authority over it (Psalm 139: 7-12). We do not know if Satan had any legal authority over the righteous souls in the Paradise section of Sheol before the Nazarene went there. Why raise this question?

Jesus did not declare that all authority was given Him in heaven and on earth until after His resurrection(Matthew 28:18; Revelation 1:18). And we do know every soul that was called back from death by priest or prophet died again, even Jesus' friend Lazarus (John 11). Before the *Resurrection of the Christ*, death appears to have had the final authority, and if so, Satan thought he had final authority in that department (Hebrews 2:14-15).

Jesus had to take away the authority (or keys) from Satan and that would take a fight. Perhaps that is one of the reasons, death is the last enemy to be destroyed, and the prison called Sheol or Hades will be destroyed as well (1Corinthian 15:26; Revelation 20:14).

We also know that Jesus had to die as the sacrifice to provide redemption for all humans that have ever lived, currently living, and will live upon the earth, even the righteous of the Old Testament that were in Paradise. It is the sacrifice of Christ on the cross and His triumphant resurrection that destroyed Satan's authority over life and death (John 10:10; Hebrews 2:10-18).

Believers in Christ can now stand their grounds and resist the devil, and he will flee. Their victory is because of the resurrection of Christ, and the in indwelling presence of the blessed Holy Spirit (Ephesian 6: 10-18; James 4:7; 1 Peter 5:8-9). Had anyone every cast out Satan before the incarnation of the Christ? We have no record of such.

For emphasis I repeat—before Jesus died on the cross, He could call back souls from Paradise as He did for His friend Lazarus and Jarious's daughter, and the son of the widow of Nain. But those that were called back all died again. So, their resurrection cannot be classified as the same as the resurrection of Jesus Christ. Those corpses were merely resuscitated or brought to life again.

They had no more capabilities than they had before they died. That signals to us that despite their coming back to life, Satan still had power over death and could kill them again, even if they were brought back a thousand times (Hebrews 2:14). Death would have had the last word.

But the Resurrection of Jesus Christ is different; it is in a class all by itself. It is the first true and permanent resurrection of a human being, because Jesus dies no more, death has no more dominion over Him (Romans 6: 9-10). For this reason, Jesus is called "the firstfruits from among the dead" or "the firstfruits of them that slept" (1 Corinthians 15: 20-23). His resurrection body is unique; it has powers it did not have before it went to the grave, such as walking through closed doors (John 20:19, 26).

Jesus had to personally fight Satan as "Spirit Being" to "spirit being" and rid him of his authority and free whatever prisoners Satan wrongly held in custody (1 Peter 3:18-22). Satan knows God's throne or kingdom is established upon "justice and righteousness" (Psalm 89:14), so Satan is quick to hold God to His own law. But Satan does not play by the rules. He was quick to point out flaws in Peter's life and demand that Jesus hand him over for discipline. Perhaps, this was Satan's attempt to setup Peter as the betrayer, but Jesus prayed for Peter to counter the Satanic plot (Compare Matthew 16: 21-23 and Luke 22: 31-34).

During His ministry in the physical body, Jesus was never alone. The Father was always with Him, and the Holy Spirit as well (Matthew 3:16-17; Luke 4:14-19). Angels assisted Him periodically (Matthew 4:11; Luke 22: 43-44). But something happened on the cross that we are not privy to without speculation, when Jesus cried out in anguish, "My God, my God why has thou forsaken me?" (Matthew 27: 45-46). Is the Nazarene mistaken? He has never made a mistake before that we have a record of—so, why now?

We do not have to go to the extreme in entertaining a rift in the Godhead. Oh no, that is radical, impossible, and heretical! But could it be that upon exiting the physical body at death, the Nazarene's "human" relationship with the Father changed? Bear in mind that like us, His physical body had weaknesses or limitations that the spiritual or resurrected body would not have. "It is sown in weakness but raised in power" (1 Corinthians 15: 42-43 KJV).

Our physical relationship with the Lord changes at death as well, but our spiritual relationship remains (Romans 8:38-39). Have you observed the change of relationship between Christ and His disciples after the resurrection?

While in the physical body Jesus had infirmities, human weaknesses (not sins) that is why He needed angels to strengthen Him. He asked the disciples to watch while He prayed. He got weary of His journey and sat on Jacob's well (John 4:4-6). He need help to shoulder the cross (Luke 23: 26; Hebrews 4:15). Remember to become incarnate, He surrendered the exercise of certain independent attributes such as omnipotence, omnipresence, and omniscience.

But something happened the moment He stepped out of the physical body at death, but we do not know what. This much we know—He was heading to Sheol for the decisive and final battle with Satan. Perhaps, He had to fight Satan by Himself with no help from the Father or the Holy Spirit or angels. It sounds good, but we cannot dogmatically insist that it was the case. We don't know!

But Satan is the kind of fellow who is quick to remind God that an action is illegal. A group of demons cried out to Jesus, do you come to torment us before the appointed time? (Matthew 8:28-29). It was a question of legality; are you here to send us hell before the appointed time, before a trial, without due process? Even Satan knows that God is just and operate in accordance with divine law. That's what the demons were asking.

In like manner, Satan could say, if the whole Godhead is ganging up on me here in Sheol, that is not a fair fight. So, your resurrection victory is not a true victory.

In Sheol, the Prince of glory was now standing One to one with the prince of darkness. For security, the Nazarene had commended His spirit into the hands of the Father as a passenger his safety in the hands of a pilot when he steps into an aircraft. The Nazarene knew He was heading for Sheol, the Paradise section for the final leg of His mission.

The Sheol visit is most critical because if He did not get out of Sheol, there would have been no resurrection, and the redemption rescue mission would have been lost. But even so, God would be no less God. Now you can see why the Resurrection of the Christ is the foundation of the Christian faith as Paul has shown us in 1 Corinthians 15.

Let us go back and pick up a line in the ministry of the Nazarene that we should address. At the very beginning of His ministry, Jesus read the following prophecy about Himself to folks at His hometown synagogue in Nazareth:

> The Spirit of the Lord is upon me, because he has anointed me to proclaim good news to the poor. He has sent me to proclaim freedom for the prisoners and recovering of sight for the blind, to set the oppressed free, to proclaim the year of the Lord's favor. (Luke 4:18-19 NIV)

As preachers and Bible scholars, most of us tend to glide over this as a prophecy from Isaiah about the Messiah, and yes, it was! But we tend to apply it narrowly to His earthly ministry of healing, delivering, and saving people. And yes, that is a correct application. But it is not limited to His ministry in Palestine and the saving work of the Church in the world; there is more that we often fail to see.

Here it is—the prophecy partly applies to the ministry of the Christ in Sheol as referenced by Peter. Look again at the quote. The word proclaim appears three times:

1) "to proclaim good news to the poor." That is to those who are destitute, powerless, and have no voice to speak up for themselves. They are at the mercy of the rich and powerful. God is always concerned about this group and made special provision for them in the Law of Moses.

2) "to proclaim freedom for the prisoner." This applies not only those Satan hold as prisoners on earth, but those in Sheol as well (that is the Paradise part of Sheol). Jesus had to proclaim liberty, redemption freedom to those in the Paradise, just as the Church and the Holy Spirit have the assignment to proclaim the gospel among the living, globally (Matthew 28:19-20; Acts 1: 8; Romans 10: 9-15).

3) "to proclaim the year of the Lord's favor." That is the Year of Jubilee when all slaves are set free. Jesus showed up in Sheol (Paradise section) to make the announcement, because Satan the slave holder was not going to do it voluntarily. He had to be compelled!

To illustrate—recall President Lincoln's emancipation declaration of Black slaves in 1863. But the good news did not reach the slaves in the Confederate States until 1865 when the Union Army showed up to enforce the declaration. The slave owners were not willing to free their slaves. Satan does not volunteer anybody's freedom. It takes a power greater than him to compel it.

So, Jesus had a mission to Sheol and that was to proclaim or announce to the souls in Paradise that the time of their redemption had come. That was good news for the saints but bad news for those who had already rejected salvation. If Paradise is in the immediate vicinity, the wicked souls could here the announcement just as the rich man could hear and know what was happening to the beggar.

The wicked souls heard the message. But there is no second chance; no repentance in the grave that holds the body or Sheol that holds the spirit. If there is, the Bible has not recorded it. So, any such doctrine must be treated as man-made and does not worth the paper it is written on.

Jesus had to win the victory in Sheol against the strong man (Satan) to be resurrected. The resurrection was the decisive blow to the kingdom of darkness and the certification of victory in favor of the Nazarene, the Prince of Glory (Psalm 24:7-10). The Resurrection was a public event with many witnesses on earth and in the heavens (1 Corinthians 15: 3-7).

In the end, we know that God the Father did not abandon the Son; that is too strong a word. At best we cannot explain this mystery; it remains classified. The secret things belong to God (Deuteronomy 29:29). All three persons of the blessed Holy Trinity participated in the Resurrection of the Christ: the Son (John 2:18-22), the Holy Spirit (Roman 8:11), and the Father (Acts 2:22-24).

But for the angelic population there was radio silence those three days in Sheol. Then on Easter morning all heaven erupted in applause and standing ovation for a job well done. If it was fitting for the angels to applaud at creation, it is even more fitting to applaud at redemption for it is the greater investment on God's part (John 3:16).

It was like the standing ovation and applause you see in NASA control centers, when the Apollo spacecraft returning to earth emerged from radio silence, from the dark side of the moon and the commander said, "Houston…The Eagle has wings." In like manner, all heaven erupted in applause and standing ovation because they knew that their Man won a decisive victory that resurrection morning. Jesus Himself said that no one can enter a strong man's house and take what he has unless you first bind the strong man (Mark 3:22-27).

The *Resurrection of the Christ* is the undisputed and compelling evidence that strong man, Satan, was decisively defeated for all times. But this does not mean, Satan is completely out of business, not at all.

It signals to us that he is greatly wounded, his power and authority greatly nullified, and God has him on a short leach. He can still bite you; he has some fighting power left but not enough to run you all over town and overcome you. Now you can stand your ground and resist him, and he will run from you (Ephesians 6: 10-18).

Satan was an archangel before he fell; it took a whole battalion of mighty angelic warriors led by Archangel Michael to put down the revolt against His Majesty's

Government and expel Lucifer (Revelation12). One person of the Godhead took him on in Sheol and beat him, reducing his power that any Holy Spirit anointed child of God can be victorious over him. Right now, he has some freedom to prowl about like a roaring lion seeking whom he may devour (1 Peter 5:8). But his power is limited.

In the end, one angel of light will serve a warrant for his arrest and bring the bad boy into custody with chains. There is a maximum-security prison prepared and awaiting him (Revelation 20:1-3).

Satan still has a role to play in the kingdom of God and Christ, but he does not know it. He thinks he is still in business for himself, so he won't quit until his usefulness comes to an end, and God throws him into the lake of burning sulfur, the final hell (Revelation 20: 7-10).

If you are still having problem about Sheol (Hades) or the underworld--the next chapter will give you a little more detail on the Hebrew thought on the matter. If you have fully grasped the concept of Sheol, then jump to Chapter 6 where the return from Paradise is discussed.

CHAPTER 5

THE BIBLICAL UNDERWORLD

We begin with the Old Testament (OT) because it gives us more information about the biblical underworld. The OT is also called the Hebrew Bible or the Tanach and it is Holy Scripture. When the apostle Paul said, "All scripture is given by "inspiration of God," the New Testament was not yet completed (2 Timothy 3:16). So, Paul was fundamentally referring to what we now refer to as the Old Testament as inspired or God breathed. The Hebrew Bible is what Jesus, and the Early Church used.

But Paul was also conscious that a New Covenant or Testament was in the making, and perhaps that accounts for him putting in writing so much of the revelation he received from the risen, glorified, and exalted Christ.

In one sense, Paul is to the New Testament what Moses is to the Old Testament. The writing of Moses constitutes a significant part of the Hebrew scriptures. In contrast, much of the New Testament was written by the apostle Paul, fourteen of the twenty-seven books, if we credit him the authorship of the epistle to the Hebrews.

None of the other apostles had a better scholarly, rabbinic command of Old Testament as the apostle Paul. In today's education, he had more than a PhD qualification. The Lord Jesus believed Paul would have been a great asset to the Church and the kingdom of God and he was. Perhaps, it is for that reason he was chosen.

There is a second way Paul is like Moses. Most of Moses writings (five books: Genesis, Exodus, Leviticus, Numbers, and Deuteronomy) were given to him directly from God by revelation, part from the oral tradition, and part his own lived experience. And so was Paul!

Yes, Paul learned some things from Peter and the other apostles, but most of Paul's knowledge about Christ and the role of the Church in the world was given to him directly from Jesus by revelation (Galatians 1:11-24). Perhaps that has something to do with him spending so much time in Arabia, about the same geography Moses received his revelation from God.[1]

Speaking of the conversion of Paul, Halley asserts that "Paul was so stunned by the stroke from heaven, and the instant realization that his whole life had been wrong, that he felt he had better think things through." This moved him to seek "solitude [in] Arabia" to reorient himself.[2] There, he received some revelations that informed his faith in Christ.

This is what I am building up to—if the Old Testament, the Hebrew Bible is the inspired word of God as Paul asserts in 2 Timothy 3:16, then it must be received as such, and on the same level with the New Testament. It must be included in Paul's "All Scripture is God breathed" statement. And historically, the Church received it as such.

Therefore, both testaments complement each other, and together constitute the complete word of God for His Church; it is inspired, authoritative, and trustworthy.

We must, therefore, accept what God has revealed about the world He created as recorded in the First Testament or Old Testament as we have come to call it. This acceptance includes Sheol (the underworld) unless God has revealed additional information to overrule or shed new light on what is written.

And this does not mean we close our eyes to what God has revealed in the book of nature and go on believing the earth is the fixed center of the Universe despite evidence to the contrary. God's book of nature complements the book of God's Word.

Jesus fully embraced the Hebrew Scriptures. He taught from it, and He quoted and affirmed the Scripture as written (Matthew 4:1-11). He warned that not even the stroke of a pen will pass from the Scripture until all is fulfilled (Matthew 5:12-20). Jesus Christ Himself is the perfect fulfillment of the Hebrew Scripture (Luke 24:13-35).

For these reasons, Jesus ratified some of the old standards and sayings based upon the new law of love that He instituted (Matthew 5:21-47; John 13:34-35). Jesus never disputed the accuracy of the Hebrew Scriptures. In fact, He chastised the religious leaders for willfully setting aside the Word of God for the "traditions of men" (Matthew 15: 1-7; Mark 7:1-15).

So, if Jesus told us He was going to Paradise and the Word of God tells us where Paradise was at the time, we should take Jesus at His word for two reasons. (1) Jesus never lied or misstated anything before. (2) He created Sheol, including Paradise, and should know where they are (John1:1-4; Colossians 1:15-17). Against this background, therefore, let us look at what the Hebrew Bible says about Sheol and Paradise.

Sheol in the Hebrew Bible

In the Hebrew and Christian Scriptures, Jesus and the Apostle, some of the Church Fathers, and several creeds of the Church speak of Christ descending into Sheol or hell, the abode of the dead.[3] Many Christian scholars stated the same, that Jesus descended to hell (Sheol or Hades). In this book, the matter is investigated so that we can give a reasonable answer to anyone who asked about our faith.

Furthermore, since the Nazarene went to Paradise with the penitent thief as He said He would; it worth looking into. Jesus was in Sheol or Paradise the three days He was out of the body. Is it important to our salvation that we know the exact location of Sheol and Paradise? The answer is no! It has nothing to do with our salvation for Jesus is already risen from the dead, and He dies no more.

But since the Old Testament Scriptures on which the New Testament relies so heavily, says so much about Sheol, it is responsible scholarship that we investigate the biblical underworld more closely.

The Biblical Underworld

Earlier, we stated that according to the Hebrew Bible, Sheol appears to be in the underworld or in another dimension or realm. And death or the underworld or both serve as the gateway to Sheol.

At least, two statements of Jesus seem to corroborate this view or at least point in this direction. (1) The story about the rich man and the poor beggar Lazarus in Luke 16:19-31. This story is not a parable. (2) Matthew 16:18 where Jesus said, "the gates of Hades [Sheol) will not prevail" over His Church. Are there other passages in the Hebrew Bible that point in this direction as well? The short answer is, there are many!

For that reason, we have selected a few to make the case. But first, we need to look at how the word "hell" is used in the scripture. At times, "grave" is used to represent hell but that is not our concern here. There are four words in original Scripture languages that are translated "hell" in the English Bible: *Sheol, Hades, Gehenna,* and *Tartaroo*.[4]

Sheol is Hebrew and is frequently used in the Old Testament to represent the underworld and is translated hell, but not the final hell. In Hebrew thought, Sheol was used to represent the "abode of the dead, not the grave, but those who have departed from this life." And that included, "both the righteous and wicked."[5] For example, "For You will not leave my soul in Sheol, nor will You allow my Holy One to see corruption in the realm of the dead" (Psalms 16: 10 NKJV).

Psalm 30:3 says, "You, LORD, brought me up from the realm of the dead; you spared me from going down to the pit" (NIV). In Isaiah 38:10 Sheol is depicted as a city with gates which recalls the statement of Jesus, "the gates of hell"(Hades) will not prevail against His Church (Matthew 16:18). What are we doing here?

We are trying to show that in Hebrew thought, Sheol refers to the underworld, a realm of conscious abode much deeper and different from the ordinary grave. In Numbers 16:28-33, the earth opened its mouth and swallowed a rebellious group led by Korah down into Sheol.

Hades is the Greek for Sheol; it is the word most frequently translated hell in the New Testament (NT), but not the final hell. Like Sheol, Hades refers to "the underworld," "the region of the departed or the dead, the intermediate state between death and resurrection."[6] Both the righteous and the unrighteous go there but they are separated as in the story Jesus told about the wicked rich man and Lazarus, the poor beggar.

The NT provides more clarity on the afterlife than the OT. Hades appear several times and it always points down or coming up. For example, in Matthew 11:23 Jesus said that "Capernaum" though "lifted up to heaven;" "will go down to Hades." In Matthew 16:18, He speaks of the gates of Hades. Again, in Luke 16:23 He speaks of the rich man looking up from Hades where he is tormented in flames.

In Revelation 1:18 Jesus said, He was dead and is alive for evermore and He has the "keys of death and Hades." Revelation 20:13-15 the sea gave up the dead that were in it, and death and Hades gave up the dead that were in them...and death and Hades were thrown into the lake of fire. The lake of fire or lake of burning sulfur is the final hell that is eternal. Temporary or eternal, Hades is a place that the Lord associates with judgment and suffering (e.g., Matthew 11:23-24; Luke 16:23-27).

Gehenna is another word that is translated "hell" in the English Bible. It refers to the Valley of Hinnom, a place where sacrifices were offered to false gods and worship of demons took place (1Kings 11:7). Later, it became a dumping site for burning garbage, including human remains (2 Kings 23:13-140.[7] The fire was constant, so in New Testament times it was used symbolically for hell to denote the eternal place of the damned after resurrection (Matthew 5: 22, 29-30, 10: 28).

The fourth word that is translated "hell" in the English Bible is *Tartaroo*. It means*, "to incarcerate" and occurs only once in the NT (2 Peter 2:4).*[8] Peter uses it to refer to wicked angels who are chained in prison in the underworld in darkness awaiting the day of judgment.

Finally, there are other underworld places spoken of in Scripture which have a hellish flavor which may or may not use any of the four preceding words. Six examples:

(1) Previously, reference was made to Numbers 16: 28-33 where the earth opened its mouth and swallowed a group of rebellious leaders led by Korah.

(2) The "abyss." This word is translated "the deep" (Romans 10:7) or "bottomless pit" and is controlled by a mighty destroying angel named Abaddon in Hebrew and Apollyon in Greek (Revelation 9:11). Revelation 11 speaks of two witnesses that God will send to preach during the Great Tribulation who will be killed by the beast that come up from the Abyss (verse 7) also Revelation 17: 8. The Abyss or Bottomless Pit is underworld. Satan will be in prison in the Abyss (Revelation 20: 1-3). There are places kept secret from humans and the Abyss is one of them.

(3) The Apostle Jude (verse 6) speaks of falling angels that are so wicked and corrupted that they are not allowed freedom of movement upon the earth as Satan has, but they are kept bound with everlasting chains under darkness, awaiting the Day of Judgment when they will be judge and thrown into hell (2 Peter 2:4; Jude 6).

(4)Sheol (Hebrew) Hades (Greek) believed to be in the underworld or in another dimension or realm.

(6) Then there is the "Lake of Burning Sulfur" which is the final hell into which Satan and all his angels and human followers, including the antichrist and the False prophet will

be thrown eternally. This includes death and Hades/Sheol, the temporary abode of the wicked souls of humans (Revelation 19:19-21, 20:7-15).

Where is the Lake of Burning Sulfur (hell)? We do not know, but if you have ever witnessed a volcanic eruption, you already know that the earth has enough firepower in its belly to accommodate all this and more. But eternal hell is much worse than what is described here, because Satan and his angels are spirit beings; natural fire as we know it, cannot destroy them. Resurrected humans, righteous and unrighteous, will also be given a spiritual body that natural fire cannot destroy (John 5:28; 1 Corinthians 15: 21-22).

Summation

In this chapter we explored the understand of the ancient people of God as it relates to the underworld. Their knowledge of the underworld revealed to them by what we consider the inspired word of God. We investigated the use of four words often translated hell : *Sheol* (Hebrew), *Hades*, *Gehenna*, and *Tartartoo* (Greek).

These four words point to the abode of the dead, a place of punishment, mostly in the underworld. Paradise in Hebrew thought, though used at times in reference to the Garden of Eden, was considered part of Sheol or located in the immediate vicinity where the departed souls were very alive and conscious (Luke 16: 22-31).

Some people will say, we live in a world driven by science, therefore, what is written in the Bible could not mean the underworld; that is how people of a pre-science world talked. But by doing that they discount what Jesus said. And He is the Creator of the Universe including the earth; He knows it better than anyone of us.

The critic says the same about the third heaven, the dwelling place of the Almighty. If God lives up there, one of our advanced telescopes would have picked Him up by now. But such thinking is ignorant. God is invisible and we only know what He chose to reveal to us.

Our best science research evidence, therefore, is the revelation of God. God could allow a thousand scientists to camp out in His living-room with their best instrument and still don't recognize His presence. We are mere mortals; when we speak of the Almighty, humility is necessary.

We do not have dogmatic certainty of the exact location of Paradise, but the OT seems to point to the underworld which could lead to another dimension or realm. The New Testament (NT) points to the heavens. The next chapter will explore the NT understanding of Paradise a little more.

We further discussed that it was necessary for the Nazarene to go to Paradise because His fight with Satan was not over. Satan appears to have had some authority over Sheol including Paradise. Jesus went there and took his authority away.

Finally, we discussed the resurrection of the Christ briefly, pointing out that it was earthshaking and powerful as His death, and that He did not return from Paradise alone according to Matthew's account. The next chapter picks up from this point

CHAPTER 6

RETURN FROM PARADISE

The *Resurrection of the Christ* is the return from Sheol and Paradise. And it was no small feat. It was a comprehensive victory, universal in scope, and eternal in length. It will never be repeated! In Chapter 4, three fundamental things are stated. They are pivotal, so we begin with them.

First, before His death, the Nazarene promised to bring the penitent thief with Him to Paradise. And He did immediately after death as promised. For security, He committed His spirit into the hands of God (Luke 23:46).

Second, according to Hebrew thought, Paradise was a part of Sheol and was located in the underworld, in another dimension or realm. Jesus confirmed not only the closeness of Paradise to Sheol (or Hades) but that the spirit of the dead are stationed there were very much alive and conscious. Furthermore, the righteous were separated from the wicked in Sheol (Luke 16: 19-31).

Third, it appears that Satan had some control over death and the souls in Sheol (or Hades) before the death and resurrection of the Christ. It was necessary, therefore, to visit Sheol to secure victory over Satan there, release the righteous, and be resurrected (Hebrews 2:14-15).

The implication of the preceding reference is that Satan had power and authority over death, elsewhere referred to as keys. Jesus fought him victoriously in the underworld and took the keys or authority from him, thus making the resurrection possible (Matthew 28:18-20; Revelation 1:18).

Without the bodily resurrection of the Christ, everything would have been lost. The resurrection is the true attestation that Jesus was not an imposter, but the Son of God as he said He was. It was the ultimate sign that He offered to the Jews who asked for a sign (John 2:18). He said to them, "Destroy this temple, and I will raise it again in three days" (John 2:19). His body was the temple of which He spoke here (Verses 20-22).

Again, the Jews asked for a sign to prove that he was the Messiah, that they could believe him. Jesus responded, "A wicked and adulterous generation ask for a sign! But none will be given it except the sign of the prophet Jonah. For as Jonah was three days and three nights in the belly of a huge fish, so the Son of Man will be three days and three nights in the heart of the earth" (Matthew 12: 38-40).

To Jesus, His resurrection was the ultimate sign of His identity as Messiah, Son of God. The resurrection is the one miraculous sign Satan cannot duplicate. That is why the apostles, and all others embrace the Resurrection of the Christ as the foundation or cornerstone of the Christian Faith (1 Corinthians 15; Ephesians 2:19-22; 1 Peter 1: 4-8).

Without the resurrection, there would have been no ascension and no exaltation. By His resurrection, our Lord Jesus Christ defeated every outpost and stronghold of evil Satan had established on earth, in the underworld, and in the heavens. Jesus conquered principalities, and powers, and thrones, and might, and dominions, including the underworld and in the heavens: atmospheric, planetary, and elsewhere (Romans 8:37-38; Ephesians 2: 1-7, 6:12).

So, the *Resurrection of the Christ* was not just a regional victory, but universal and comprehensive. It exalted Him to the highest position of authority, above all creatures (Philippians 2:8-11; Hebrews 1:1-4). God cannot be exalted above God nor a creature exalted above God. God is not a creature because He is not a created being; He is self-existent. We now analyze the return from Paradise with this understanding as the framework.

He Returned with the Saints

The first thing to note is that the Nazarene did not go to Paradise alone and He did not return alone. He went with the penitent thief, and He returned with the Old Testament (OT) saints that were in the Paradise part of Sheol. Some people ask, "Why is that?" And that's a good question.

The sacrifice of Christ on the cross as the Lamb of God, reached back as far as Adam and Eve, to cover their sins.

Because animal sacrifices offered for sin in the OT were a temporary fix; they could not permanently atone for sin (Hebrews 10:1-14). The life an animal is not equal to the value of human life, but there was no other alternative.

If God took the life of each sinner, He would destroy the entire race because all have sinned. That approach would be counter-intuitive, even if He had destroyed Adam and Eve the moment they sinned. He would still destroy the whole human race in them. It would defeat the purpose of creating humans. The approach He took is not only one of love and compassion; it is most ingenious. He continued with His original plans and in time became incarnate and pay the debt Himself (Genesis 3:15; Galatians 4:4-7).

So, animal sacrifice was a temporary fix until the true sacrifice came to atone for sin permanently. The splitting of the veil in the temple the moment of Christ's death, was the signal that animal sacrifice was forever ended, and the *Resurrection of the Christ* its confirmation.

The Temple in Jerusalem was the only place where sacrifice could be offered to God. Its destruction in AD 70 was the final nail in the coffin of that sacrificial system. That destruction was prophesied by Jesus during the week of His passion (Matthew 24:1-3). Animal sacrifice is no longer required by heaven for sin. Jesus was and is the sacrifice.

You might be hearing for the first time that Jesus Christ did not walk out of Sheol and the tomb alone but with a vast multitude of saints; that may be a surprise to you. It is not a popular preaching topic, because there are not many Scripture passages directly addressing this issue.

But there are strong implications from several scripture passages pointing in that direction, and there is at least one passage that addresses the issue head on. So, let's take some time to address the issue from the direct passage and from the implication passages.

First, the direct scripture passage. It takes us back to Golgotha the day Jesus died, that first Good Friday. Matthew gives us this intelligence report:

> And Jesus cried out again with a loud voice, and yielded up his spirit. Then, behold, the veil of the temple was torn in two from top to bottom; and the earth quaked, and the rocks were split, and the graves were opened; and the bodies of the saints who had fallen asleep were raised; and coming out of the graves after His resurrection, they went into the holy city and appeared to many. (Matthew 27: 50-52 NKJV).

Some scholars see the passage as controversial, because it lumps two main events together: the crucifixion and the resurrection. But the passage is not controversial in itself; the controversy is imposed by scholars who find the events too spectacular to accept.

Matthew simply describes the crucifixion and the extraordinary phenomenon that took place at that time. The earth quaking, stones split into pieces, the curtain of temple torn from top to bottom, graves burst open. Then he said, and the "bodies of the saints that were asleep raised; and came out of their graves after the resurrection." Note the time they came out of their graves not at the time of the crucifixion but [at] the resurrection.

The other gospels (Mark and Luke) confirmed most of the upheaval that occurred in nature during the crucifixion of the Christ: the darkness, earthquake, rocks moving out of their places, and the curtain of the temple rend in two from top to bottom, but they do not include graves being opened. But that is the very reason we have four gospel accounts; what one does not include, the others may.

Matthew states that at the very moment of Jesus' death "graves were opened," but note that no one came out at that time. The implication is that the path was clear for them to come out. The narrative goes on to say, "and the bodies of saints who had fallen asleep were raised; and coming out of the graves after His resurrection…." Who came out of their graves? Saints (the righteous ones) who had fallen asleep (died). When? After or at the resurrection of the Christ. If the souls of the saints that were asleep came back from Paradise at the crucifixion, there would hardly be a reason for Jesus going to Paradise or Sheol. Jesus went to Paradise because of them.

The resurrection of the Christ was an earthshaking phenomenon as His death was earthshaking. Matthew (28:1-3) says there was a "violent earthquake for an angel of the Lord came down from heaven and going to the tomb, rolled back the stone and sat upon it." The Roman soldiers on guard were knocked down, fall on their faces like dead men. These hardened soldiers were scared straight. Upon regaining their composure, they fled from the scene and reported what happened to their superiors who concocted a false story and bribed the guards (Matthew 28: 11-15).

So according to Matthew's account, saints that had fallen asleep were raised with Jesus and came out of their graves on the morning of Jesus' resurrection. If that be the case, these are the souls from Paradise in the region of Sheol where Jesus and the repentant thief were the three days Jesus was out of the body.

Again, bear in mind that all the Old Testament saints were waiting for the sacrifice of Jesus Christ, the true Lamb of God, and He went to them to announce the good news. It makes sense, therefore, that Jesus would not leave them there but bring them with Him from that underworld place, region, or realm. But are there any other scripture that points in that direction?

Second, scriptural implications—these are passages that indirectly point in the same direction of the Matthew passage. One such passage is Ephesians 4:7-13. Here, the apostle Paul speaks of Christ descending to the lower regions of the earth and then ascended to heaven, taking with him those who were in captivity (verse 8).

Some scholars do not consider this passage to mean Christ descended to the underworld. So then, the passage has two schools of thought. One says, it refers only to Christ coming to earth; the other says, it means more than that, it refers also to His descent to Sheol, the underworld, Paradise section. This author takes the latter position.

The apostle Peter also asserts that Christ went to the region or abode of the souls of the departed and preached or announced the good news of redemption to them (1 Peter 3:18-20). The passage is very compelling, but some scholars still don't consider it to mean that Jesus went to Sheol or Hades or Paradise. But remember that Jesus Himself said He was going to Paradise. Peter is merely confirming His reason for going there, to announce that the day of their redemption has come, and by extension to lead them out of there.

In Bible times, when a warrior defeated his enemy, he always brought back people who were taken captives or as prisoners of war and the spoils of war would be shared among the soldiers and gifts given. An example of this is when Abraham returned from the slaughter of the ten kings who raided Sodom and took his nephew, Lot and his family (Genesis 14:17-24).

The men that went with Abraham, 318 of them, shared the spoils of the victory of war. Abraham refused the offer of the king of Sodom who represented the evil one (Satan). But note that Abraham's victory was given to God; it was celebrated sacramentally with the mysterious personality known as Melchizedek. He brought bread and wine and received tithes from Abraham. Tithes is God's share.

Melchizedek is a type of Christ (Hebrews 7). Under the New Testament (NT), we too sacramentally celebrate the victory of our Lord Jesus Christ with bread and wine. We call it the Lord's Supper or Holy Communion. We also have Easter service to celebrate His resurrection.

A second example of a victorious warrior sharing the spoils of war and sending gifts is King David. This he did when he won the victory over the Amalekites. They burned Gilgal and took David's family, the families of his men, and all their belongings. With the help of God, David recovered everyone and everything (1 Samuels 30: 21-31). The spoils of the victory were shared equitably with the men who were too exhausted to joint the fight, and gifts were sent to others and thanks to God (verses 24-26).

On resurrection morning, Jesus came back as a mighty warrior over Satan, death, the grave and Sheol. And thousands of souls were with Him according to Matthew's record. This is what the apostle Paul said with regards to Jesus the warrior returning and giving gifts to His people:

> But to each one of us grace has been given as Christ apportioned it. This is why it says: When he ascended on high, he took many captives and gave gifts to his people. (What does he ascended mean except that he also descended to the lower, earthly region? He who descended is the very one who ascended higher than the heavens, in order to fill the whole universe). So, Christ himself gave the apostles, the prophets, the evangelists, the pastors and teachers, to equip his people for works of service, so that the body of Christ may be built up….(Ephesian (4: 7-13).

Note that Jesus came from the lower region of the earth with those who were captives, and that he ascended on high and gave gifts to His people just as warriors did before and during His earthly ministry.

The question now is this—what has happened to these souls that came out of their graves and Paradise with Jesus on resurrection morning, that first Easter? We will address this question in the next chapter. For now, we want to address the issue of time change.

The Resurrection Signals a New Age

The *Resurrection of the Christ* ended one Age and started another. It ended the present age that Jesus was born into—that is, the age of law and animal sacrifice; and the new age of grace began. This does not mean God's Law is no longer applicable, nor does it mean grace was not operable before. Grace and law have always been at work since creation and will continue to the *New World Order*.

After the Fall, Adam and Eve were treated graciously; "Noah found grace in the eyes of the Lord (Genesis 3: 21-22, 6:8). The Law is fulfilled in Christ but not destroyed. Some laws have been ratified and some ceremonial ones ended (Matthew 5:17-48). But the law of God is now summarized under Christ's new law of love and is written inwardly on the hearts of humans by the blessed Holy Spirit (Mark 12:28-31; John 13:34-35; Hebrews 8: 8-12).

The indwelling Holy Spirit makes it possible to keep the law of God in the Age of grace by practicing the law of love.

The ancient people of God used to speak of three ages: the past age, the present age, and the age to come. The present age is the Church Age; it runs from the Day of

Pentecost (Acts 2) to the *Second Advent of the Christ*. After that will be what some scholars call, Kingdom Age.

The Bible also speaks of the last days, which is a period of time that runs from the Resurrection of the Christ to the end of the Final Judgment (Revelation 20:7-15). In the context of her brother's death, Martha said to Jesus, "I know [my brother] will rise again in the resurrection at the last day." Jesus responded, "I am the resurrection and the life. The one who believes in me will live, even though he dies, and whoever lives by believing me will never die…"(John 11:24-26 NIV).

This Lazarus, a close friend of Jesus, died and his soul went to Sheol (Paradise section). Jesus demonstrated His power and authority over death by calling him back to his physical body after he was dead four days (John 11:43-44). This happened before Jesus went to the cross, so Lazarus coming back to life was not in the same category as the Resurrection of Jesus, because Lazarus died again, as well as all others that were raised.

But Jesus after His resurrection dies no more; "death has no more dominion over Him" (Romans 6: 8-10). His Resurrection body, though recognized as the same body, had capabilities it did not possess before, such as walking through closed doors, able to vanish at will, and not recognized at times. This is the type of resurrection body the people of God will receive at the end of the Church Age (John 5:28; 1 John 3:1-2; 1 Corinthians 15: 35-56).

The unrighteous will also be resurrected but not at the same time as the righteous (Revelation 20:11-15). For more on resurrection, see Volume 8 by this author in the series, "Related Events to the Second Coming of the Christ." Let's try to remain focused here.

So, Jesus went to Paradise and came back. The three days that He was out of His physical body, where was He? Jesus told us in advance where He would be. He once said, "As Jonah was in the belly of the big fish three days and nights, even so must the Son of Man be in the heart of the earth three days and three nights" (Matthew 12:40).

Some scholars take this to mean the grave, but the grave is a shallow place and in no way classified as the heart of the earth. Paul tells us that Jesus descended into the lower regions of the earth (Ephesian 4:7-9). Again, some scholars take that to mean the grave.

As He was exiting the body at the time of death, Jesus committed His spirit into the hand of His Father (Luke 23:46). And He went to Paradise as He said He would to the penitent thief. Wherever Paradise is, in the underworld, another dimension or realm; He said he was going to Paradise that very day of His death (Luke 23:42-43).

All the righteous souls in Paradise were redeemed by the sacrifice of the Lamb of God on the cross. They were looking forward to the cross as we now look backward to the cross. Peter tells us that Jesus descended into Sheol and preach to the souls in prison who were disobedient during the time of Noah (1Peter 3: 18-20). Scholars again find this passage difficult and conflate it. But it is not that difficult if we take all the information together.

We already established that it is in the underworld or another dimension or realm, and that it has at least two compartments according to the teachings of Jesus in Luke 16: 19-31; part for the righteous souls and part for the unrighteous. Since there is no hope of repentance after death, preaching to them would be futile.

The part of Sheol Jesus must have gone is the compartment that is called Paradise. He told the penitent thief on the cross that He was going to Paradise that very day of His death, and the thief would accompany Him.

The passage from Peter tells us He went there. We already know that the unrighteous in their compartment can hear and see what is going on in Paradise. So, if Jesus were preaching or announcing the good news of the gospel for the redemption of those in Paradise. The wicked souls in their compartment could hear the gospel that they rejected that cause them to be in that place of torment. But it was now too late to get out of there. Now they were able to see and hear the one whom they rejected when the gospel was preached in their lifetime whether by Noah, Moses, or any of God's prophets.

The unrepentant thief arrived in Sheol that very day as well but not in the Paradise section. And just as the rich man could look across Paradise and recognize Lazarus, the beggar, at Abraham's side, the unrepentant thief could hear and see Nazarene and the penitent thief by His side. But they are separated by a great gulf fixed between that there is no getting across from one side to the other.

If that underworld space is no longer used to house the souls or spirits of the departed righteous, what is it used for, and where do righteous souls go now? This is a compound question; the latter part is answered in the next chapter. The answer to the first part, as to the use of the space, I don't know. But The answer in the following paragraph has been suggested.

The answer is almost comical, but this is too serious a matter to be flippant about. Everything in the Word of God is written for a purpose and should be taken seriously. The prophet Isaiah speaking of God's judgment upon backslidden Israel said, "Sheol has enlarged its appetite and opened its mouth beyond measure, and the nobility of Jerusalem and her multitude will go down..." (Isaiah 5:14).

Taken literally, the verse is saying one of two things: 1) the grave has enlarged itself, or 2) Sheol, the place of departed spirits has enlarged herself. If you take the second meaning, the implication could mean, the compartment of Sheol that was called Paradise is now used to accommodate just the souls of the unrighteous. This interpretation could be a stretch, but Jesus said broad is the way that leads to destruction, and many are on their way there (Matthew 7:13 ESV).

CHAPTER 7

THE TRANSFER OF PARADISE

P aradise has not only been lost and regained; it has been transferred to another place. Historically, it has been strongly believed and understood by the Church that Sheol or Hades remain a prison for the wicked souls who have departed this life. But Paradise has been transferred from its pre-resurrection, Old Testament (OT) location, to somewhere in the heavens. Stated another way, the risen Christ has transferred the righteous souls from Sheol to a Paradise in the heavens.

While we will not seek to dogmatically establish this position, we assert that the New Testament scripture strongly points in this direction. So, let us take some time to briefly unpack this scenario. We will seek to answer three questions: when did paradise move? Where has it moved to? And what has become of the space it once occupied? This last question is already answered.

Now, no one needs to die defending this hill because it has little or nothing to do with your salvation whether you believe one way or the other.

When Was Paradise Transferred?

Paradise is more than a geography; it is a condition of bliss and hope. So, by transfer we mean the relocation of those souls that were enjoying bliss as opposed to torment. The contrast is laid out in the story of the rich man and Lazarus.

There were millions like these two, experiencing one condition or the other, depending on which part of Sheol they were located: hell, or Paradise. The victory of Jesus in Sheol is a resurrection victory which resulted in the release of the souls in Paradise. The geography is still there but the residents are gone; they left with Jesus. It is believed by some that Sheol has enlarged herself to accommodate a greater multitude of wicked souls as the population of the earth increases (Isaiah 5:14, 14:9).

According to Matthew, Jesus showed up with the residents of Paradise on resurrection morning. We do know they were relocated somewhere in the heavens, but went? There are two time slots to choose from: 1) immediately after the resurrection of the Christ, or 2) forty days after, at His ascension (Acts 1:9-11). The immediate position has minimal scriptural support; the forty-day position has none. We will examine both.

First, the immediate position. Matthew (27:52) states, "The bodies of many holy people who had died were raised to life. They came out of their tombs after the Jesus resurrection and went into the holy city and appeared to many people."(NIV). If we accept the Word of God to be inspired, authentic, and reliable, then we are compelled to accept this as written, no matter how spectacular.

Matthew is telling us, Jesus was not resurrected alone, a multitude came out of the tomb with Him. Since, He was coming from the Paradise part of Sheol where He visited the Old Testament saints, this crowd could be no other than OT saints (1 Peter 3: 18-20). Jesus went to Paradise because of them, that be the case, there would have been no reason to leave them in Sheol (Paradise section).

The evidence, though a little weak, shows that the immediately transferred to Paradise somewhere in the heavens is more likely than not, but why?

Jesus was on a mission to earth and His resurrection is the success and official completion of that mission. The first thing He would likely do is report to His Father who commissioned Him. At least, that is what we would do. But did Jesus do that?

We do not really know because the evidence is not compelling enough. But there are strong scriptural clues in favor of the immediate position. We will examine the four gospel accounts of the resurrection for evidence that Jesus went to heaven before he showed Himself to His disciples. Mark is believed to be the first gospel written, but we will examine them as they appear in our Bibles.

Matthew said, "Mary Magdalene and the other Mary" were the first to arrive at the tomb (Matthew 28:1). But the resurrection had already taken place; an angel at the site told them, "He is not here; he has risen, just as he said. Come and see the place where he lay. Then go quickly and tell his disciples. He has risen from the dead and is going ahead of you into Galilee. There you will see him" (vv.5-7).

On their way to report the angel's message and their findings to the disciples, Jesus met them in person, thus confirming the message of the angel that He is risen (vv.8-10). It is fair to say, Jesus had enough time to make a trip to heaven and back, but we have no evidence of that.

Mark's account confirms Matthew's, that the women were the first to be at the tomb, but Mark named three women: Mary Magdaline, Mary the mother of James, and Salome (Mark 15:1). Mark's account also confirm that the resurrection had already taken place when the women arrived. The stone was already rolled away from the tomb.

Mark also reports that the women saw an angel (a young man) who told them the Lord was risen and heading for Galilee, and they need to go tell his disciples and Peter (vv. 2-8). Again, it is fair to say, Jesus had enough time for a trip to heaven and back before he revealed Himself to His disciples, but we have no evidence of it.

Luke's account confirmed both Matthew's and Mark's accounts. The women first arrived, found the stone rolled away, and Jesus gone from the tomb, angels confirmed that Jesus is risen and where the disciples could find Him (Luke 24:1-10). Still no evidence that He went to Heaven.

Now we look at John's account (John 20). John only name Mary Magdalene coming to the tomb early that morning. Finding the stone rolled away, she ran back to tell Simon Peter and John; they ran to the site, witnessed it for themselves, and returned to the place they were staying. Mary Magdaline, who had returned to the tomb after telling Peter and John, stood at the grave weeping.

Then she stooped down to take another look into the tomb. This time she saw two angels: one at the head, the other at the feet, where the body of the Lord was lain. They asked her, "Woman why are you crying? Who is it you are looking for?" (John 20:15).

Believing she was speaking to the gardener she responded, "Sir, if you have carried him away, tell me where you have put him, and I will get him." Upon saying that, a voice responded from behind her saying her name, "Mary." She turned to see who it was—it's Jesus! She cried out in Aramaic, "Rabboni!" (which means, Teacher) (John 20:15-16).

Now, picture the excitement. Bear in mind this is Mary Magdalene. She was there at the cross, watching Jesus until He was dead. She and the other women followed Nicodemus and Joseph of Arimathea with the body of Jesus to the tomb so they could mark exact location (Matthew 27:57-61; John 19:38-42).

Jesus was dead for three days and nights and now He is back calling her by her name. This is the critical point we having been building up to, so note Mary's interaction and Jesus' response to her in this first resurrection encounter.

In her excitement, Mary held on to Jesus as if she would never let Him escape from her again. Jesus had to pry her loose while saying, "Do not hold on to me, for I have not yet ascended to the Father. Go instead to my brothers and tell them. I am ascending to my Father and your Father and to my God and your God" (John 20:17-18).

Bible commentators tend to emphasize the first part of the statement, "I have not yet ascended" because it is easier to work in the Acts (1:19-11) ascension. But they ignore the second half that says, "I am ascending" which suggests immediate action.

There are only two ways to understand these words of Jesus: 1) while Mary was taking this good new message to the disciples, Jesus went to heaven to report to His Father. Or 2), the statement is forward looking to His ascension which would happen forty days later.

Second, the forty-day position. This position maintains that despite what Jesus said to Mary, He did not return to heaven until His ascension in Acts (1: 9-11). If you take this position, your first difficulty is what Jesus said to Mary in that first encounter. The second difficulty is—where is the vast multitude of saints that came back with Him, were they roaming around Jerusalem for forty days? The third difficulty is—Jesus ascended to heaven public to His followers, about 120 of them. They saw Him ascended alone; no multitude was with him (Acts 1:9-11).

The More Plausible Position

We have looked at two positions to when did Jesus relocate the Old Testament saints who came out of the tomb with Him on resurrection morning? Immediately or forty days later at the Mount of Olives Ascension? Both positions have problems and are difficult to defend, but the scripture points more favorably to the immediate position. There are three points of plausibility.

First, the scripture points in that direction. Jesus said He was heading for heaven to His Father. That took place before showing Himself to the disciples.

Second, His resurrection body could have made that journey in the blink of an eye and back to debrief his disciples for forty days.

Third, going to heaven at this time would be the more appropriate time to settle the souls that came out of the grave with Him to their Paradise home above. Again, you don't need to lose friends defending this position; we already admit that it is weak.

The Relocation of Paradise

It is commonly accepted in the Church that since the resurrection of the Christ, Paradise has been relocated to somewhere in the heavens. This means the souls of the righteous who departed this life, no longer goes down to Sheol or Hades, but up to God. This is strongly supported in the New Testament. For example, "For to be absent from the body is to be present with the Lord" (2 Corinthians 5:6).

The apostle Paul uses the word *Paradise* to describe a place in the third heaven to which he was caught up. He could not say whether he was in or out of the physical body when it happened. But there in Paradise he received revelations that he could share with the people of God, but he also saw and heard things that were classified; he was not permitted to disclose (2 Corinthians 12: 1-4).

Other than the apostle John, no other apostle received the quantity and quality revelations as Paul received. Mysteries that were hidden in God from ages past were made known to Paul. Most of the hidden knowledge shown to him were about the person of Christ, the gospel, the kingdom of God, redemption, the Church, and the relationship of the Church to Israel (Romans 1:16-18; Galatians 1:11-12; Ephesian 1:9-14, 2:19-22; Colossians 1: 25-27). The examples are too numerous to list here.

Because of the quantity and quality revelation given to Paul, God had to keep Paul humble, less he exalt himself beyond measure. The apostle informs us that due to the "surpassingly great revelations…I was given a thorn in my flesh, a messenger of Satan, to torment me" (2 Corinthians 12:7). A messenger of Satan is an angel of Satan, a demon.

God allowed this demon to follow Paul around and stir up trouble for him to keep him humble. Three times he pleaded with God to call off this dog, but God said, no. "My grace is sufficient for you, for my power is made perfect in weakness" (2 Corinthians 12: 8).

Paul is not the only one who was caught up to the third heaven where, it appears, Paradise is located. The apostle

John was invited to come up, and was raptured through an open door to heaven, into the throne room of the Almighty Himself. John's description of what he saw in heaven is awe-inspiring (Revelation 4-6).

John also saw the Lamb of God, the second person of the blessed Holy Trinity there (Revelation 5:5-14). Most of the content of this last book of the Bible was given to John from here by Jesus Christ. But he also assigned an angel who escorted him through heaven.

There are other scripture passages pointing to the third heaven as the possible location for Paradise. For example, the church at Ephesus that had lost its first love for Christ, was scolded to repent and do its first works over. The Lord said to them, "…to the one who is victorious, I will give the right to eat from the tree of life, which is in the paradise of God (Revelation 2:7).

Revelation 6:7,16:7 reveals the souls of the martyrs under the altar in heaven crying out to God to avenge those who had violated them. These are the souls of people who were slain for the word of God. Bible scholars often say these are *Great Tribulation martyrs*, but they may very well be martyrs from all ages, Old and New Testament.

The preceding passage, therefore, stands as further affirmation that the souls of departed righteous people no longer go down to a paradise in Sheol but to Paradise in the heavens, and this is since the Resurrection of the Christ. Charles Wesley's classic hymn, *"Christ the Lord Is Risen Today"* (1739) gives this ever so relevant line:

Love's redeeming work is done, Allelula!

Fought the fight, the battle won, Allelula!
Death in vain forbids Him rise, Allelula!
Christ has opened paradise, Allelula!

Wesley is affirming what every Christian now knows, that without the resurrection redemption would have been incomplete, death would have won, and paradise closed.

The Full Restoration of Paradise

Bible scholars are right, Paradise began in a garden, the garden of Eden, and it was lost in a garden (Genesis 3). The travail of the Nazarene in a garden (Gethsemane), strengthened Him for His sacrifice on a cross and His triumphant resurrection. In the words of John Milton, *Paradise Lost* has become *Paradise Regained*.

The Bible closes with humankind occupying the fully restored Paradise. We know because Jesus tells us the tree of life is in the Paradise of God (Revelation 2:7). The tree of life that was in Eden is here, but this time it is in the City of God (Revelation 22:1-4, 14).

Summation

The story of the humankind began in a garden, commonly referred to as the Paradise Garden because it was blissfully perfect until an intruder breached the hedges, and Paradise was lost as suffering, death, and the prospect of hell rushed in to fill the vacuum.

THE TRANSFER OF PARADISE

But centuries later, and man dying on the gallows on a hill call Calvary, flanked with two thieves, one on His right, the other on His left was destined to visit Paradise.

At first both thieves joined the chorus of the mob to hurl insults at the man dying on the middle gallows; they said, "…come down from the cross, if you are the Son of God!" Save yourself, come down from the gallows and save us too (Matthew 27:38-44).

But amidst the insults, one thief observed a difference with the man on the middle gallows, he seemed innocent. With that he changed side and signal to his partner in crime that this man between us both is innocent, be careful what you say to him; He might just be who He said He is, the Son of God. Even with that warning his companion kept on cussing the Nazarene to his last breath.

The penitent thief had shifted his attention to the man beside him on the middle gallows. He said to Him, "Remember me when you comes into your kingdom." The Nazarene responded, "Truly I tell you, today you will be with me in Paradies" (Luke 23: 32-33, 39-43)

Both men breathed their last and stepped out of their bodies, and their spirits went together to paradise in a region of the underworld called Sheol or Hades.

The man on the middle gallows was the Son of God, the Savior of humankind, the one to conquer Satan, and death itself. He freed a vast multitude in Sheol (the Paradise section) and led them out to eternal freedom to the Paradise above in the heavens.

Paradise is fully restored and better than it was before. The story of humankind begins in a garden and will culminate in a garden in a city (Revelation 22:1-5). On second thought there will be no end to Paradise this time; the bliss will be eternal.

We humans are like the two thieves, the Savior is right there with us in our seemingly hopeless predicament, and we may or may not recognize His presence. But now you know His is there, so like the penitent thief, you can call on Him for help. When you do, you will change destination to an eternally better place.

REFERENCES

CHAPTER 1

1. Constantinou, Eugenia Scarvelis. THE CRUCIFIXION OF THE KING OF GLORY. *The Amazing History and Sublime Mystery of the Passion.* Chesterton, IN: Ancient Faith Publishing, 2021, (p.247).

2. Ibid, (pp.217-222).

CHAPTER 2

1. Constantinou, Eugenia. *The Crucifixion of the king of Glory*, (pp.214-217).

2. Spence, H.D.M., Excell Joseph S. Editors. *The Pulpit Commentary.* Vol.16 (St. Luke 23.32). Grand Rapids MI: Wm. B. Eerdmans Publishing Company, 1978 (P.239).

CHAPTER 4

1. Buttrick, George Arthur. Editor. Interpreter's Dictionary of the Bible Dictionary Vol.3 (K-Q). New York: Abingdon Press, 1962 (p.655).
2. *Ibid.*

CHAPTER 5

1. Unger, Merrill F. and Harrison R.K. Editor. *The New Unger's Bible Dictionary*. Chicago, IL: Moody Bible Institute, 1988 (p.91).
2. Henry H. Hally. *Halley's Bible Handbook*. Deluxe Edition. Grand Rapids, MI: Zondervan, 2007 (p.723).
3. Holcomb, Justin S. *Know the Creeds and Council* .Grand Rapids, MI: Zondervan, 2014, p.25.
4. *The New Unger's Bible Dictionary.* (p.550).
6. *Ibid.*
7. *Ibid.*
8. *Ibid.*

OTHER BOOKS BY THIS AUTHOR

  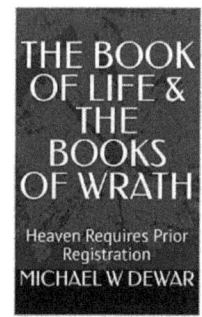

Series: *Related Events to the Second Coming of the Christ* (10 Volumes).

Vol.1　　　　　Vol.2　　　　　Vol. 3

Vol. 4
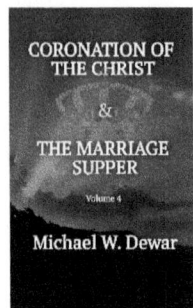

Vol. 5

Vol. 6
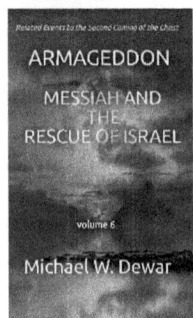

Vol. 7

Vol. 8

Vol. 9

Vol. 10

ABOUT THE AUTHOR

Michael W. Dewar, Sr. is a pastor, Bible teacher, and a mentor in the spiritual life for more than forty years. He is also a specialist in the resolution of church and family conflicts. He is the author of a three-volume course of study in church conflicts, and how to launch a peace ministry in your local church.

He holds advanced degrees from several institutions of higher learning including the Master of Divinity, the Master of Social Work, and an earned doctorate.

Reverend Dewar is the founder and pastor of the New York Congregational Baptist Church (NYCBC). He lives with his family in New York. He is the author of the 10-Volume series, *Related Events to the Second Coming of the Christ.*"

Destructive Conflict Can Destroy your Church.

Don't allow it! Launch a peace ministry in resolution of conflict at your local church with this course of study.

Textbook

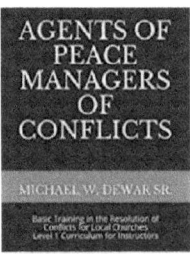

Instructor's Manual

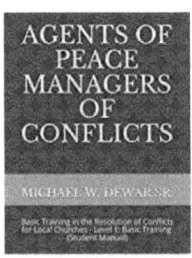

Student's Manual

www.ingramcontent.com/pod-product-compliance
Lightning Source LLC
Chambersburg PA
CBHW071721040426
42446CB00011B/2167